Learning About
CULTURES

Literature, Celebrations, Games and Art Activities

by
John Gust, M.A.
and
J. Meghan McChesney

illustrated by Marilynn G. Barr

Teaching & Learning Company
1204 Buchanan St., P.O. Box 10
Carthage, IL 62321

Cover by Skjold Photographs

Copyright © 1995, Teaching & Learning Company

ISBN No. 1-57310-012-9

Printing No. 9876543

Teaching & Learning Company
1204 Buchanan St., P.O. Box 10
Carthage, IL 62321

This book belongs to

_____

Acknowledgements

We would like to extend a heartfelt thanks to those individuals who have helped to make this book a reality:

To our students at Kelly Elementary School in Compton Unified School District and Compton Avenue Elementary School in Los Angeles Unified School District for testing these activities and challenging us to become better teachers.

To Kevin McChesney, who will undoubtedly be a fantastic teacher in his own right.

To "Gram" (Joyce Metzler), whose cookies are always full of love.

To Stephen Schaffzin for providing activities and advice on Judiasm.

To Don and Judy Mitchell, Bob Steinman and Jill Eckhardt at the Teaching & Learning Company for your unwavering support and allowing us the opportunity to write this book!

Dedication

To the children of every culture.

Table of Contents

Dear Teacher or Parent,

When first presented with the idea of integrating multicultural education in the classroom, some teachers may moan at the idea of teaching yet another subject. Teachers have enough to worry about as it is, right? Absolutely! We believe that incorporating multicultural activities in your class will actually make your job easier. Would you like to know how? Then read on!

Multicultural education covers all areas across the curriculum—language arts, social sciences, math, science, art, physical education, music and more. After all, doesn't every culture read, write, record their history, build communities, add, subtract, multiply, divide, experiment, observe, paint, draw, build, create, run, jump, skip and sing? Of course! Well, then integrating multicultural activities should be easy since you're already teaching all these curricular areas. Multicultural education simply supplies you with a few new ways of doing so. And we've made it simple for you by providing all the resources you will need—focusing on literature, games, art and celebrations.

Still you may ask, "But why is it important to teach multicultural education?" As you undoubtedly know, schools in the United States are becoming increasingly more diverse. The number of minority students is growing, as is the number of children with different religious and familial backgrounds. If we believe in educating all children and helping to make these diverse students feel welcome in our classrooms, then it becomes essential to address their needs. But this isn't an argument only for children with "special interests," all children need to be exposed to other cultures. Because, not only are our schools becoming more diverse, but so is our society—regionally, nationally and globally.

We are quickly becoming a global society. The ever-expanding role of technology is fostering the breakdown of the ethnocentric, racial and national boundaries that we are familiar with. This expansion of technology allows us, and our students, to be in contact with more people around the world on a daily basis. The world our children will live in as adults will incorporate technology and communication and global interaction in ways that we cannot now even contemplate. For this reason alone it becomes imperative for students today to interact and become familiar with the people of various cultures from all around the globe.

Your students absolutely need a multicultural education to successfully survive and thrive in their community, within our nation and on a global scale. If we desire to tackle the problems in this world, then we will need to work together. Working together begins by understanding and appreciating our similarities and differences! This is what multicultural education is all about. We need to help our students respect and become tolerant of these disparate views, while not forgetting the overriding similarity—we're all people!

Under the right circumstances, all students are eager to learn. Taking your students on a trip around the world without leaving your classroom will spark curiosity and create engaged learners. Invite your students to climb aboard your magic carpet for a ride that they will remember and use for the rest of their lives. You and your students can visit the people and the cultures in many not-so-distant lands by using this resource as your guide.

Sincerely,

John Gust and J. Meghan McChesney

African American Culture

African Americans comprise one of the largest ethnic groups in our country. American society has been heavily influenced by the culture and personalities of African Americans. Human history begins in eastern and southern Africa, where evidence of the first human beings has been found. The history of African Americans begins in ancient Africa where the kingdoms of Mali, Ghana and Songhai left a legacy of literature, art and music. Today, African culture continues in many diverse forms across the 50 independent countries on the continent. Over 3,000 ethnic groups who speak more than 1,000 different languages contribute to the cultural and ethnic traditions that influence people all over the world, particularly the United States. While most African Americans cannot trace their family history to specific countries in Africa, their historical roots stem from central and west Africa where these kingdoms flourished.

African Americans were held in captivity in the United States for more than two hundred years and yet they developed a culture and community spirit that thrived. The myths that supported the African slave trade were expressly designed to create the false impression that Africans were subhuman and lacked the structures of European civilization. African Americans have played important roles in shaping the history and culture of the United States during the Civil War, Reconstruction, the Harlem Renaissance, desegregation and the Civil Rights Movement. Notable African Americans include Harriet Tubman; Malcolm X; W.E.B. DuBois; Martin Luther King, Jr.; George Washing-ton Carver and Sojourner Truth.

African Americans' lasting contributions to the history and culture of the United States is particulary impressive considering their limited rights and denial of the ecomonic, social and political gains which other citizens have enjoyed. African Americans today still struggle to reclaim their past traditions and to forge a strong, positive identity for their culture which has been discriminated against for much of the history of this country. An appreciation of African and African American traditions will help your students understand the strengths of these two great cultures.

African American Culture

Literature

Abiyoyo by Pete Seeger (Macmillian)

African Dream by Eloise Greenfield (Thomas E. Crowell)

Aio, the Rain Maker by Fiona French (Oxford University Press)

Amos Fortune by Elizabeth Yates (Dutton)

Anansi the Spider by Gerald McDermott (Holt, Rinehart, and Winston)

Ashanti to Zulu by Margaret Musgrove (Dial Press)

The Black Snowman by Phil Mendz (Scholastic)

Bringing the Rain to Kapiti Plain by Verna Aardema (Dial Press)

Chicken Sunday by Patricia Polacco (Philomel)

Children of the Sun by Jan Carue (Little, Brown & Co.)

Cornrows by Camille Yarbrough (Coward-McCann)

Darkness and the Butterfly by Ann Grifalconi (Little, Brown & Co.)

The Drinking Gourd by F.N. Monjo (HarperCollins)

Edgar Allan by John Neufeld (Phillips)

Flossie and the Fox by Patricia McKissack (Dial Books)

Follow the Drinking Gourd by Jeanette Winter (Knopf)

Half a Moon and One Whole Star by C. Dragonwagon (Aladdin Books)

The House of Dies Drear by Virginia Hamilton (Collier Macmillan)

Iggie's House by Judy Blume (Bradbury)

Jafta by Hugh Lewin (Carolrhoda Books)

Jamaica-Tag-Along by Juanita Havill (Houghton Mifflin Co.)

Ji-nongo Nongo Means Riddles by Verna Aardema (Four Winds)

Kwanzaa by A.P. Porter (Carolrhoda Books)

M.C. Higgins, the Great by Virginia Hamilton (Macmillan)

Mirandy and Brother Wind by Patricia McKissack (Knopf)

Mufaro's Beautiful Daughters by J. Steptoe (Lothrop, Lee & Shepard)

Not So Fast, Songololo by Niki Daly (Atheneum)

The Patchwork Quilt by Valerie Flournoy (Dial Books)

A Picture Book of Martin Luther King, Jr. by D. Adler (Scholastic)

Roll of Thunder, Hear My Cry by Mildred Taylor (Dial)

Sam by Ann Scott (McGraw)

Scorpions by Walter Myers (Harper)

The Snowy Day by Ezra Jack Keats (Viking)

Soul Looks Back in Wonder by Tom Feelings (Dial)

Sounder by William Armstrong (Harper)

Stevie by John Steptoe (Harper)

Sweet Whispers, Brother Rush by Virginia Hamilton (Philomel)

Tell Me a Story Mama by Angela Johnson (Orchard Books)

Why the Sun and the Moon Live in the Sky by E. Dayrell (Houghton)

Why Mosquitoes Buzz in People's Ears by Verna Aardema (Dial Books)

Celebrations

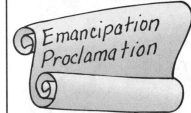

Emancipation Proclamation

On January 1 we celebrate the anniversary of President Lincoln signing the Emancipation Proclamation freeing slaves.

Kwanzaa

African American families celebrate this cultural holiday created by Dr. Maulana Karenga between December 26 and January 1.

Dr. Martin Luther King Jr.'s Birthday

Martin Luther King was born on January 15, 1929. Many churches and synagogues around the country hold memorial services to honor MLK. King's most famous peaceful demonstration was the march that he and 200,000 followers took from the Washington Monument to the Lincoln Memorial in 1963. It was there King delivered his famous "I Have a Dream" speech.

Emancipation Day

Abraham Lincoln read the Emancipation Proclamation on September 22, 1862.

National Black History Month

In February we celebrate the contributions of famous African Americans such as Langston Hughes, Thurgood Marshall and others.

Harambee Day

During the last week in October we celebrate this day which means, "Let's all pull together."

National Freedom Day

On February 1 we celebrate the abolition of slavery in the U.S. which occurred in 1863.

Springbok

In southern Africa there is an animal similar to a gazelle named the springbok. This game is played by having one child imitate the actions of a Bushman hunting a springbok. First have all your children form a circle holding hands. Pick two players, with one being the "hunter" and the other being the "springbok." Put both players into the center of the circle and blindfold them both. Then spin both players around to get them disoriented. Have one student who is part of the circle announce that the hunt has begun. Once the hunt begins, the hunter's job is to move as quietly as possible in order to catch the springbok. Naturally, the springbok's job is to avoid being caught by the hunter. Players in the circle can make animal noises to help distract the hunter. When the springbok has been captured by the hunter, the game is over. Two new players can enter the circle. If the hunter does not catch the springbok after an adequate period of time, assign a new hunter to try to catch the elusive springbok.

Nine Men's Morris

This game is sure to be a success in your class since it has been played around the world since 1400 B.C. Nine Men's Morris originated in an ancient Egyptian temple in Africa and was then carried around Europe by traders from Greece and Phoenicia. The game is easy and fun to play, and the gameboard can be readily drawn on the ground or a piece of paper.

What you will need to teach this game to your students is a copy of the Nine Men's Morris Gameboard and 18 playing pieces, nine each of two different colors, for each pair of students. This game is played with two people. Nine Men's Morris is a game of thinking and planning. The object of the game is to form lines of three markers in a row in order to capture your opponent's pieces. To start the game, each player takes a turn at placing one piece on the gameboard until they have placed all nine of their pieces. Once all of the pieces are on the board, players move their pieces one at a time along any straight line to an adjacent empty spot. As each player moves, they try to line three pieces in a row. When three pieces in a row have been lined up, player may capture any opponent's piece that is not part of a row of three. A piece can only be taken from an opponent's row of three if no other pieces can be captured. To win the game, a player must capture all but two of their opponent's pieces or block their opponent so that they cannot move. Watch your students scheme to get their pieces into the correct strategic position!

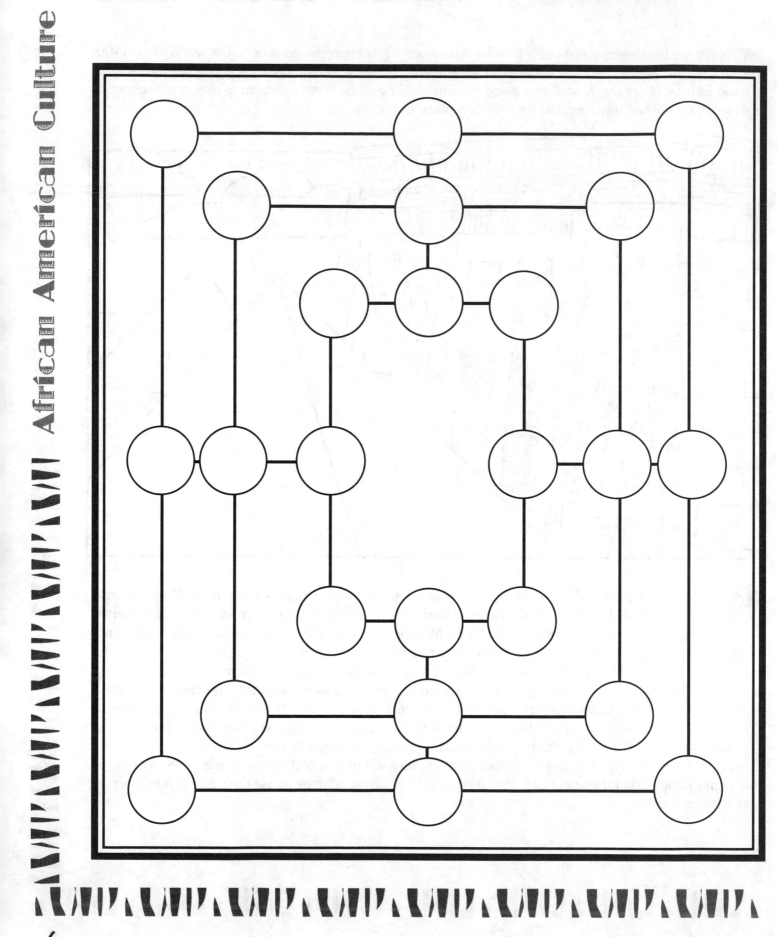

Peoplemids? What's a Peoplemid? Well, have you ever heard of a pyramid? Of course you have. Here's a way to re-create the Great Pyramid of Giza, only slightly smaller. If you'd like the Peoplemid true-to-scale of the pyramid in Africa, you'll need 2,600,000 students, give or take a few. That's approximately how many stone blocks it took to construct the great pyramid in Egypt. We recommend Peoplemids of only 10 students each. Four large-sized people on the bottom, three medium-sized people for the middle row, two small-sized people for the upper middle row and one extra-small brave soul for the top position. You'll want to make sure that your students have a soft landing pad in case of any poor construction methods. A tumbling mat or grassy area should do just fine.

If your students really become interested in the whole idea of Peoplemids, or rather pyramids, you may want to check out the book *Pyramid* by David Macauley (Houghton Mifflin). Students may choose to generate their own self-directed research, or you may wish to provide the book for a great silent-reading alternative.

Kufi Hat

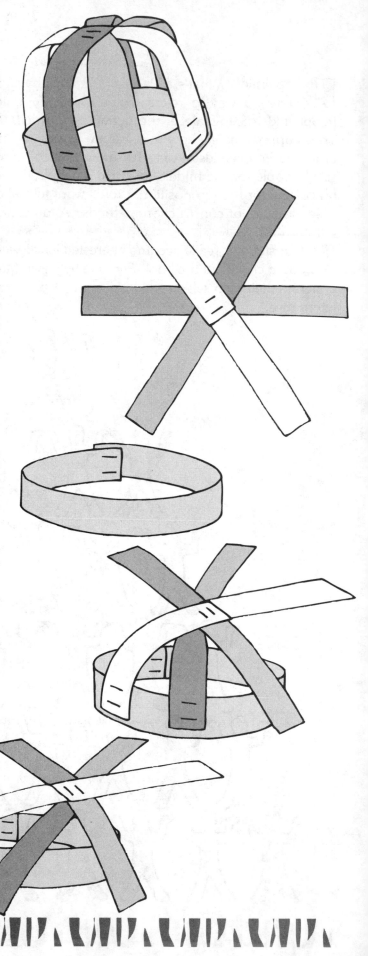

We can all show pride in the African American culture by wearing a traditional hat called a Kufi (pronounced KOO-fee). Sometimes the hat is made of a brightly colored cloth called Kente (KEN-te), but for our purposes the use of construction paper in bright colors will be sufficient.

Materials

Give each student six strips of brightly colored construction paper. Let your kids have a variety of colors to choose from (yellow, green and red usually work best), and make the pieces 12" (30 cm) long by 1" (2.5 cm) wide. Also give each student one piece of dark–colored construction paper 24" (61 cm) long by 2" (5 cm) wide.

Procedure

1st: Have your students arrange the six pieces of brightly colored construction paper as if they were the spokes of a wheel. Then staple all six pieces of paper together in the center.

2nd: Wrap the larger piece of dark-colored construction paper around each child's head so that it fits snugly, and then staple the ends together.

3rd: Have your students attach the ends of brightly colored construction paper to the dark-colored headband. Do this by stapling one strip at a time to the outside of the headband. Once your students have stapled the first one, the rest are easy.

Symbolic Sponges

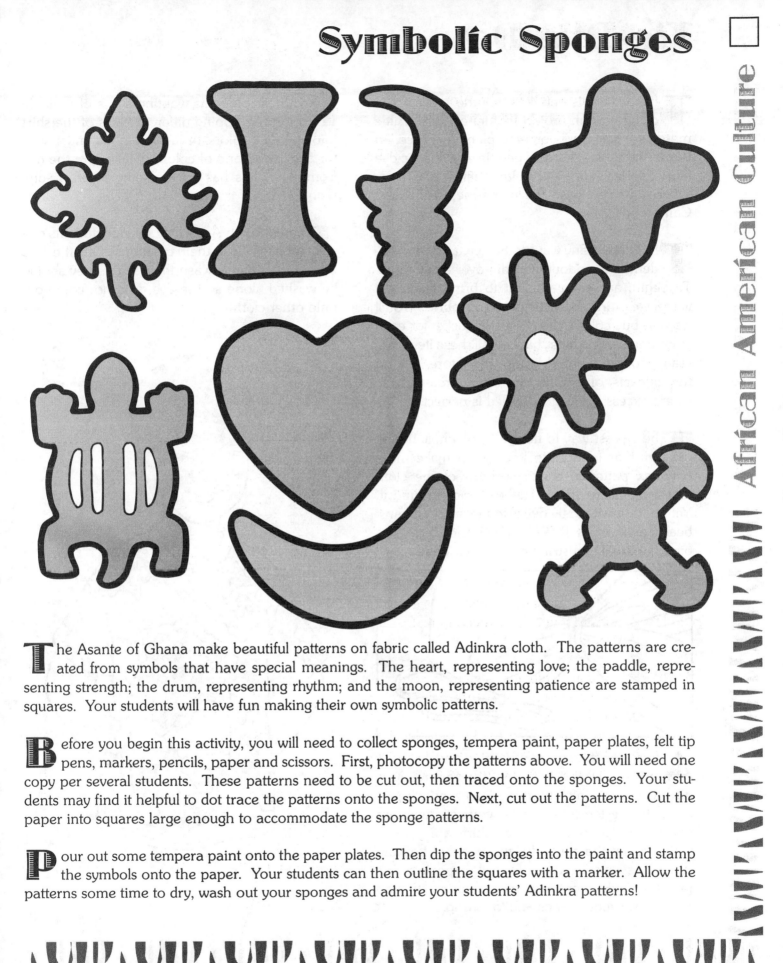

The Asante of Ghana make beautiful patterns on fabric called Adinkra cloth. The patterns are created from symbols that have special meanings. The heart, representing love; the paddle, representing strength; the drum, representing rhythm; and the moon, representing patience are stamped in squares. Your students will have fun making their own symbolic patterns.

Before you begin this activity, you will need to collect sponges, tempera paint, paper plates, felt tip pens, markers, pencils, paper and scissors. First, photocopy the patterns above. You will need one copy per several students. These patterns need to be cut out, then traced onto the sponges. Your students may find it helpful to dot trace the patterns onto the sponges. Next, cut out the patterns. Cut the paper into squares large enough to accommodate the sponge patterns.

Pour out some tempera paint onto the paper plates. Then dip the sponges into the paint and stamp the symbols onto the paper. Your students can then outline the squares with a marker. Allow the patterns some time to dry, wash out your sponges and admire your students' Adinkra patterns!

9

Tie-Dye Day

This activity is definitely for the brave. Tie-dying is a fun project that tends to be a little messy, so make sure you have plenty of space. In West Africa, the Yorube people call the tie-dye fabric, adire. Adire is popular in Nigeria, Ghana, Liberia, Ivory Coast, Sierra Leone, Benin and Cameroon.

There are many ways to tie-dye, and your students will undoubtedly discover a few more. To begin, ask every student to bring in an old white tee shirt, socks or piece of fabric. You'll need to buy colored fabric dye, a bucket for each color and some rubber bands. All these items are readily found at your local grocery store. Set up the buckets of dye in an open area—outside where excess dye can be spilled is perfect.

The easiest way to tie-dye is to simply tie the shirt or fabric into knots. To make more complex patterns, bunch sections of the cloth together and wrap the rubber bands around it. Yet another way to tie-dye is to put stones, beans, beads or marbles in a pouch in the shirt, then bind the area with string or a rubber band.

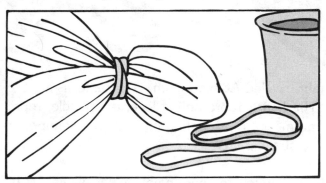

After your students have twisted and tied their shirts to their satisfaction, they are ready to dip their shirts into the dye. Restraint will produce the best results. Once your students are covered in dye, or rather their shirts are covered with dye, let the shirts dry thoroughly. Leaving the shirts out in the sun will expediate the process. Only after the shirts have dried, unwrap the knots, rubber bands and/or string.

For those students wanting shirts of multiple color, try dipping different parts of the shirt into alternate colors, or just re-dip the entire shirt for a kaleidoscope of colors. Make sure the dye from prior dips has dried slightly before re-dipping.

Then have an Adire Day so your students can proudly wear their creations! Oh, the first time your students wash their shirts, they should be washed alone so the dye does not come out onto other clothing.

Arabic Culture

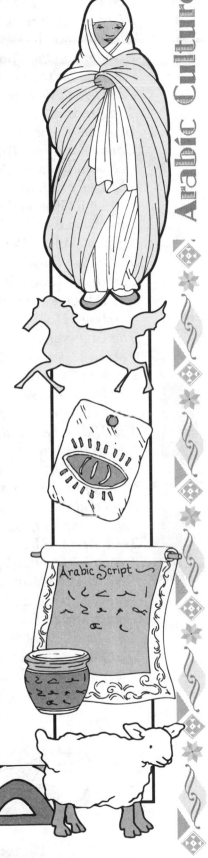

Arabs? Who are Arabs? The word has an uncertain origin, but probably means "those who speak clearly" or "those who speak Arabic." In the 7th century, when the Arabian Peninsula was united by the religion of Islam, the name *Arab* spread in its usage. The different tribes, for the first time, adopted a common identity that included religion, law and language. These people have been united ever since. Today, the Arab world consists of the people on the Arabian Pensinsula, as well as people in nothern Africa and southwestern Asia. There are 19 nations in the Arab world. They are Algeria, Bahrain, Egypt, Iraq, Jordan, Kuwait, Lebanon, Libya, Mauritania, Morocco, Oman, Quatar, Saudi Arabia, Sudan, Syria, Tunisia, the United Arab Emirates, Yemen (Aden) and Yemen (Sana). All of the 100 million Arabs in the world consider their ancestral home to be the Arabian Pensinula where their most sacred shrine, the Grand Mosque in Mecca, is located.

There is perhaps no cultural group today that arouses more emotion or intolerance in America, and other Western countries, than the Arabs. Due to the many violent events in the Arab nations, these feelings are to some extent understandable. However, the conflict between Arabs and Western countries is not new. Basically, it stems from the very old boundary between Christianity and Islam. And in our time, the major source of struggle has been due to the Western support of Israel, which Arab nations have harshly opposed.

Because of this conflict, many inaccurate perceptions and negative stereotypes of Arabs prevail. Images of gun-carrying terrorists, money-hungry oil barons and scheming sheiks with harems of captive women often come to mind. It is for this reason that we need to take responsibility in teaching our students who Arabs really are.

Literature

Abdul by Rosemary Wells (Dial)

Abdul's Treasure by Susan Mosley (Hodder and Stoughton)

Aladdin and His Wonderful Lamp by Sir Richard F. Burton (Delacourte Press)

Aladdin and the Enchanted Lamp by Marianna Mayer (Macmillan)

Ali Baba and the Forty Thieves by Walter McVitty (Abrams)

Arab-Israeli Wars by Ken Hills (Marshall Cavendish)

The Arabs in the Golden Age by Mokhtar Moktefi (Millbrook)

Bedouin by John King (Raintree Steck-Vaughn)

Count Your Way Through the Arab World by J. Haskins
     (Carolrhoda Books)

The Day of Ahmed's Secret by Florence Heide and
     Judith Gilliand (Lothrop, Lee & Shepard)

Deserts by Richard Stephen (Troll Associates)

Egypt by Valerie Weber (Gareth Stevens)

The Flying Carpet by Marcia Brown (Scribner's)

Fortune by Diane Stanley (Morrow)

A Gift for the King by Christopher Manson
     (Henry Holt)

The Gulf War by John King (Dillon)

Kassim's Shoes by Harold Berson (Crown)

Libya by Richard Tames (Watts)

The Magic Horse by Sally Scott (Greenwillow)

Mecca by Shahrukh Husain (Dillon)

The Middle East and Africa by Robert Ingpen (Chelsea House)

Middle Eastern Food and Drink by Christine Osborne (Bookwright)

Nadia the Willful by Sue Alexander (Pantheon)

Oasis of Peace by Laurie Dolphin (Scholastic)

Sami and the Time of the Troubles by Florence Heide (Clarion)

Take a Trip to Egypt by Keith Lye (Watts)

Take a Trip to Iran by Richard Tames (Watts)

Take a Trip to Iraq by Richard Tames (Watts)

Take a Trip to Morocco by Keith Lye (Watts)

Take a Trip to Saudi Arabia by Keith Lye (Watts)

Take a Trip to Syria by Keith Lye (Watts)

Terrorism by Elaine Landau (Lodestar/Dutton)

Two Pairs of Shoes by Pamela Travers (Viking)

The Young Black Stallion by Walter Farley
   (Random House)

Celebrations

Arab League's Establishment Anniversary

On March 22 this political holiday is observed in many Arab nations. The Arab League is an organization created to promote Arab unity.

Ramadan

This fast is held in Moslem countries beginning on the first full moon in late summer/early fall. Once this full moon is seen, Moslems do not eat, drink or smoke from sunup to sundown for one month. Instead, they spend this time praying in mosques in remembrance of Mohammed. Moslems believe that this fast enables the soul to rest and to be developed. The fast ends on the next full moon with the Eid ul-Fitr festival.

Islamic Festival of Eid ul-Fitr

This festival ends the month of fasting called Ramadan. *Eid* means "happiness," and *ul-Fitr* means "breaking the fast." During these three days, families go to the mosques to pray, prepare feasts, go to fairs, visit friends and give and recieve presents.

St. Barbara's Day

This Christian-Lebanese holiday celebrated in November is similar to Halloween in that children dress up in costumes and masks and go begging for treats.

Eid ul-Adha

This religious holiday is the festival of sacrifice which commemorates Abraham's willingness to sacrifice his only son Eshmael on God's command. On this day, children wear new clothes and a lamb is sacrificed.

The Fox's Tail

This game emanated from a time when Arab shepherds were watchful of the ever-present danger of the hungry fox. First, you will need a large cloth handkerchief. Once you have a handkerchief, tie several large knots into it. Students hold hands and form a big circle. Once the circle has been formed, have your students sit down. The players sitting in the circle will be the shepherds. Choose one player to be the fox. While holding onto the knotted handkerchief, the fox's job is to run around the outside of the circle several times chanting as loud as he can, "The fox goes round and round!" The shepherds sitting in the circle are to respond with the words *And on his tail there are some knots!* After several chants, the fox should gently tickle one shepherd in the circle with the handkerchief or "fox's tail." The tickled player must then quickly get up and chase the fox around the outside of the circle. If the fox is tagged before reaching the shepherd's place, then the shepherd becomes the new fox. If the shepherd is not fast enough, then the fox continues to tease the shepherds sitting in the circle.

The fox goes round and round.

14

Mancala was first played in Egypt by the Pharaohs over 3,000 years ago. Wow, that's a long time ago! Your students will be intrigued by this game of strategy, skill and foresight.

For this game, you will need to reproduce the gameboard provided and gather 32 beans or stones for each pair of students playing the game. The object of this two-player game is to collect as many stones as possible before the opponent clears all the stones from her side of the board.

Here's how to play. Two players sit facing each other with the reproducible gameboard in between. Instruct each player to claim the row of small bins on their side of the gameboard and the larger scoring bin, or mancala, to their right. Have each player place four stones in each of their smaller bins. To start the game, the first player picks up all the stones in one of the small bins. That player should then distribute the stones counterclockwise by putting one stone in each bin, including her own mancala bin. Remember the object of the game is for each player to collect the most stones in their mancala, so make sure players don't place any stones in their opponent's mancala! If the player places the last stone that she took from one of her bins in her own mancala, she earns another turn. If the player places a stone in an empty bin on her side of the board, then she captures all of her opponent's stones in the bin directly opposite of her empty bin. She then places all the captured stones, plus her "capturing" stone in her mancala. The game ends when one player clears all of the stones from her side of the board. When this occurs, the other player places all the remaining stones on her side of the board into her own mancala.

As players become proficient at playing the game, they will learn that it is not always wise to be the first player out. To win the game, the player must have the most stones. If a player is ready to go "out" and his opponent has more stones in his mancala, then he needs to find a way to stay in the game. The player with the most stones wins!

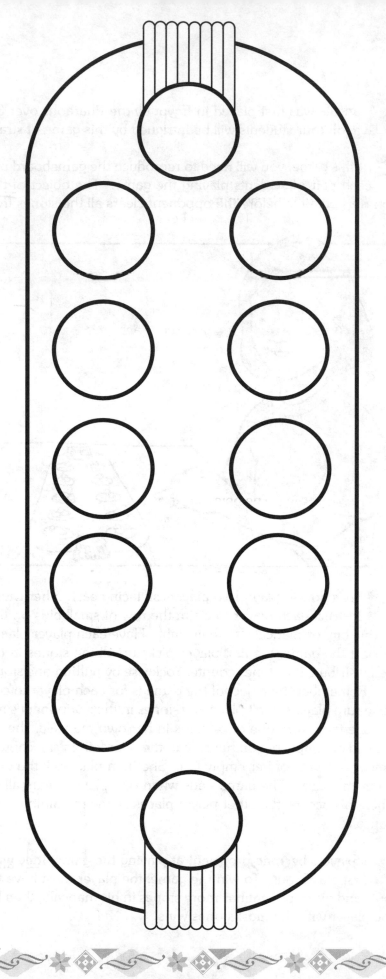

Arabic Culture

Once your students have mastered Mancala, they may want to try their thinking, planning and strategy skills on Wari. This game, which is a variation of Mancala, is also thousands of years old and is played in many Middle Eastern and African countries. The gameboard is usually made from a carved log, although this game can easily be drawn on dirt or sand.

Egg cartons are an easy way to replicate the carved wood gameboard—although you're welcome to try carving a log yourself! Each pair of students playing will need an egg carton and 48 playing pieces. If your students desire, they can decorate their gameboard with paint, markers and construction paper.

Here's how to play. Two players sit facing each other with the gameboard in between them, just like Mancala. Each player owns the six cups closest to him. The object is to win the most playing pieces.

To begin playing, each cup is filled with four playing pieces. The first player takes all the pieces from any cup on his side and distributes one piece into each of the next four cups, counterclockwise. Players alternate turns, choosing and redistributing playing pieces. If the player places his last playing piece in an opponent's cup that contains two or three pieces, the player captures all of those pieces *and* the pieces in the two adjacent cups that also have two or three pieces. Captured pieces are stockpiled on the side of the board.

Here are a few extra rules. If a player places a piece in a cup that contains 12 or more pieces, the player must "sow" those pieces at the end of her turn. The player places one piece in each cup, always skipping the cup that they were taken from. If all of a player's cups are empty, and the opponent can't fill them, then the player wins all of the pieces on the board.

To win the game, just capture the most pieces and be the first to empty all of the cups. Your students will have fun scheming!

Amulets

Most teachers have mastered the "evil eye," a look intended to freeze even the most disruptive child on the spot. In all Arab countries, people shared the belief that harm could be done by casting a similiarly menacing glance. To ward off the power of these glances, Arabs wore protective devices called amulets, or silver ornaments, around their necks. Since the first glance of the evil eye was considered to be the most harmful, these amulets were displayed prominently to catch the maliciousness intended for the wearer. If you visited an Arabic country today, you could still find people wearing amulets, although the meaning for the more educated has become less significant.

Your students may have cast the "evil eye" without even knowing it! Looks of envy are considered to be one form of the evil eye. To help your children understand the Arabs' beliefs, ask your students if they have ever felt jealous or envious of a brother or sister, a friend's new toy or clothes, or a classmate's schoolwork. Perhaps they feel jealous about a friend's talents. Once your students have discussed their emotions, they will be ready to design their amulet.

For this activity, your students will need rolled aluminum which is heavier than aluminum foil and can be bought in art supply stores. In addition, they will be using one piece of paper, scissors, a pencil, string or yarn and beads. For starters, have your children design a symbol for their amulet on a piece of paper. They may want their symbol to relate to an object or trait that they covet, or they may just want to draw an evil-looking eye. Their designs should be the size of a necklace charm. Remind them to include a hole for the string. Next, have your students place their drawings on top of a piece of the rolled aluminum. Carefully trace the design, pressing down hard with a pen. Their design will be transferred onto the aluminum. Now have your students turn the aluminum over. With their pencil, they can trace the details from the back to create a relief on the front. Next, have your students cut out their amulet and punch a hole through the top for the string. The edges may be a little sharp, so you may want to have your students file, bend over or cover the edges with tape. You be the judge. Remember, safety first. Finally, string beads and the amulet on the yarn. Your students now have their own Islamic silverwork and a charm that can ward off the most evil of eyes–including yours!

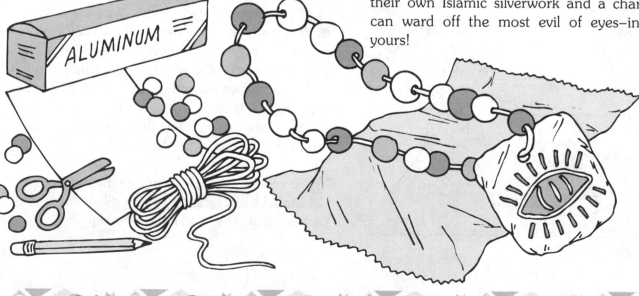

Arabic Name Design

Here's a chance to have your students learn a little Arabic. Arabic is a Semitic language spoken by over 200 million people worldwide. The Arabic alphabet consists of 12 symbols which can be combined into 28 consonants. The vowels, unlike English, are indicated by distinguishing marks above or below the consonants. Arabic is written and read from right to left, so their books begin at the "end" from your students' perspective. The letters look elegant in script and have become a developed art form in Arab countries. Calligraphy is found on buildings, pottery, textiles and books. The Koran, or holy book of Islam, contains beautiful examples of the Arabic script.

After reading to your class, *The Day of Ahmed's Secret*, by Florence Heide and Judith Gilliand, your students will enjoy learning how to write *Ahmed* in Arabic while designing their own name card.

To make Arabic name designs, each student will need the Arabic Name Design reproducible (page 20), construction paper, crayons, scissors and glue. First, have your students fold the reproducible in half. Next, instruct your students to write their name below Ahmed's in script. Then have them cut along the top side of Ahmed's name. Once completed, allow your students to display their ornate name card on their desk for the day. Using the paper cutout, ask your students to glue Ahmed's name to a piece of construction paper. Finally, have your students decorate the name design using the Arabic letters provided. Your students now have two beautiful pieces of Arabic artwork!

Arabic Name Designs

Follow your teacher's directions to make a beautiful Arabic name card and name design. Below are the 12 symbols from the Arabic alphabet and Ahmed's name. Use the symbols to decorate the design.

Arabic artists have developed a unique art form of rich and sophisticated linear designs and geometric patterns. This type of art grew from the Islam religion's forbiddance of creating pictures of people with the Arab perference for idealized, rather than natural forms. Art that consists of natural forms contains flowers, leaves and plants, while art in an idealized form consists of simple shapes such as triangles, squares, circles, hexagons and pentagons. These shapes are skillfully repeated to create beautiful patterns.

You can introduce this art form to your class through picture books such as *Aladdin and His Wonderful Lamp* by Sir Richard F. Burton. *The Magic Horse* by Sally Scott or *Abdul's Treasure* by Susan Mosley. After sharing the illustrations in these books, your class will have a better understanding of decorative art. Make sure you point out the whole pattern, the parts in the pattern, the relationships between the parts and the colors used in each motif.

Your class can create their own stencils for Arabic art using tagboard, construction paper, scissors, pencils and crayons and the Stylin' Stencil Shapes reproducible (page 22), watercolor paint and brushes are optional. To begin, prepare 4" x 4" (10 x 10 cm) squares of tagboard for your students' stencils. Have your students draw circles, squares, triangles, hexagons and pentagons within the tagboard. Have them carefully cut out each shape. Several shapes have been provided on the reproducible for those students having difficulty drawing geometric forms. The piece of tagboard, not the cutout, is the stencil. Now have your students place their stencils on a piece of white construction paper. Using crayons or watercolors, color or paint over the stencil. Encourage your students to create a pattern similar to the illustrations in the picture books, not just random shapes on the paper. By changing the shapes and colors, your students should be able to create a geometric pattern.

Stylin' Stencil Shapes

Here are some simple geometric shapes that you can cut out and trace onto the tagboard squares that your teacher has given you. Then you will be ready to create some stylin' stencil designs.

Chinese Culture

So you want to teach your students about China and its rich culture? Here are some fascinating facts that your students will be intrigued to know.

- The Chinese civilization and culture is over 5,000 years old, which means that the Chinese people have had a common culture longer than any other people on Earth!

- The Chinese people were governed by a dynastic system for several centuries. If this had occurred in Europe, the same form of government would have lasted from the Roman Empire until the 20th century, and the same cultural system and language would be shared by all people in Europe today. The Chinese system was abondoned for Communism within the last 50 years.

- Chinese writing is almost 4,000 years old, which means people in China have been readers and writers 50 times longer than people have been living in the United States.

- More than 1 billion people live in China, which makes it the most populated country in the world.

Chinese people did not start immigrating to the U.S. in large numbers until the Gold Rush in California in the late 1840s. These Chinese immigrants came to do menial labor, not to search for gold. Chinese immigrants continued to come to the West through the end of the century. Some stayed, some returned to China. Due to the shortage of workers at that time, the Chinese were welcomed into the gold mines, lumber mills, fisheries, canneries and on migrant farms. Many opened their own businesses. And of course, the transcontinental railroad would not have been built without the Chinese immigrants' hard labor. As more European Americans moved West and began to compete with the Chinese Americans for jobs, people with anti-Chinese sentiments campaigned for the denial of naturalization privileges and restrictions on the numbers of immigrants permitted to enter the country. These rights were not restored to Chinese–Americans until the 1940s when China became an American ally in World War II. Today, Chinese Americans still face discrimination, although they are becoming increasingly appreciated for their scientific and artistic contributions to the United States and for their delicious ethnic food!

Literature

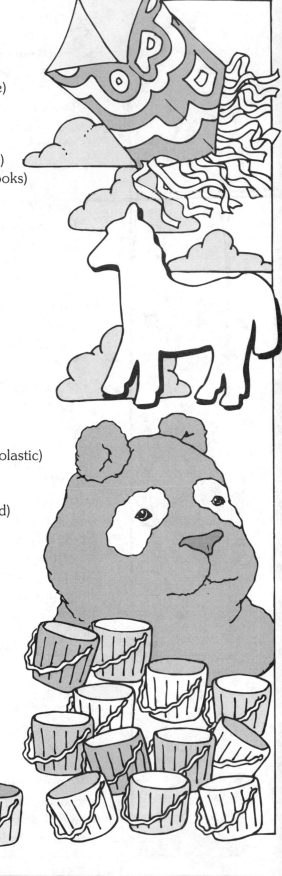

Chang's Paper Pony by Eleanor Coerr (Harper)

Chen Ping and His Magic Axe by Demi (Dodd, Mead & Co.)

Child of the Owl by Lawrence Yep (Harper)

Children of the Yangtze River by Otto S. Soend (Pelham Books)

Chinatown Sunday, the Story of Lillia by C.A. Bales (Reilly & Lee)

Chinese by Jodine Mayberry (Watts)

The Chinese-American Experience by Dana Wu (Millbrook)

Chinese New Year by Tricia Brown (Henry Holt & Co.)

Chin Chaing and the Dragon's Dance by Ian Wallace (Atheneum)

Count Your Way Through China by Jim Haskins (Carolrhoda Books)

Elaine, Mary Lewis, and the Frogs by Heidi Chang (Crown)

El Chino by Allen Say (Houghton)

The Enchanted Tapestry by Robert D. San Souci (Dial Books)

Emma's Dragon Hunt by Catherine Stock (Lothrop)

The Emperor and the Kite by Jane Yolen (World)

Eyes of the Dragon by Margaret Leaf (Lothrop, Lee & Shepard)

A Family in China by N.L. Fyson and R. Greenhill (Lerner Pub.)

The Golem & the Dragon Girl by Sonia Levitin (Dial)

Grandfather Tang's Story by Ann Tompert (Crown Publishers)

Gung Hay Fat Choy by June Behrens (Children's Press)

Her Own Song by Ellen Howard (Atheneum)

I Hate English! by Ellen Levine (Scholastic)

I.M. Pei by Pamela Dell (Children's Press)

The Iron Moonhunter by Kathleen Chang (Children's Press)

Lion Dancer: Ernie Wan's Chinese New Year by K. Waters (Scholastic)

Lon Po Po by Ed Young (Philomel)

The Lost Garden by Laurence Yep (Messner)

The Lunimous Pearl: A Chinese Folktale by Betty Torre (Orchard)

Michael Chang by Pamela Dell (Children's Press)

The Mountains of Tibet by Mordicai Gerstein (HarperTrophy Books)

The Princess and the Sun, Moon, and Stars by B. Reuter (Pelham Books)

Roses Sing on New Snow by Paul Yee (Macmillan)

The Seven Chinese Brothers by Margaret Mahy (Scholastic)

The Star Fisher by Laurence Yep (Morrow)

Tales from Gold Mountain by Paul Yee (Macmillan)

A Thousand Pails of Water by Ronald Roy (Alfred A. Knopf)

Tye May and the Magic Brush by Molly Bang (Greenwillow Books)

The Weaving of a Dream by Marilae Heyer (Puffin Books)

When Panda Came to Our House by H.Z. Jensen (Dial Books)

Yang the Youngest and His Terrible Ear by Lensey Namioka (Little)

Yeh-Shen, a Cinderella Story from China by A.L. Louie (Philomel)

Celebrations

Chinese New Year (Yuan Tan)

This Chinese holiday is celebrated on the first day of the new moon which varies from January 21 to February 19. The Chinese celebrate this day to show their appreciation for the previous safe and happy year and to wish for another properous year to come. The first day of this religious and historical celebration is dedicated to worshipping ancestors and Buddha and to praying for happiness, prosperity and good fortune. The following 14 days are filled with parades, fireworks, gift giving, feasting and dancing.

Dragon Boat Festival (Dyun Ngn Jit)

Celebrated in China on June 24, this festival is the official beginning of the summer season. On this day, the Chinese honor the memory of the popular and outspoken statesman and poet Ch'u Yuan by acting out a search for his body. Ch'u Yan drowned himself after an important prince accused him of being dishonorable. Today boats shaped like dragons reeenact the efforts to save Ch'u Yuan's life.

Lantern Festival

Celebrated on the last day of the New Year celebration, people carry lighted lanterns in a huge parade on the way to a carnival. At the head of the parade is the enormous Golden Dragon, the Chinese symbol of goodness and strength. These dragons are sometimes 100 people long! Evil spirits are warded off by fire, loud noises and the color red; firecrackers give off the perfect BANG!

Children's Day

On April 4 children who have achieved excellence in academics, citizenship or extracurricular activities are honored.

Moon Festival

On the 15th day of the 8th month (which means September 15 or 16 according to the Chinese calender), the moon is thought to be at its brightest. On this day the Chinese, like Americans on Thanksgiving, give thanks for the harvest. A large, round and yellow moon cake is made and eaten.

Ching Ming

This holiday celebrates the arrival of spring in early April. Picnics, tree-planting ceremonies, sacrifices of food and money are made in memory of deceased ancestors.

Chinese Tangram

☐

The tangram is a fascinating puzzle that originated in China more than 4,000 years ago. According to one legend, a Chinese scholar named Tan dropped a ceramic tile that he was carrying to the emperor. While trying to repair the broken tile, Tan discovered that the pieces could be used to make shapes, pictures and designs. Both children and adults love to play with this puzzle consisting of seven pieces–five triangles, one square and one rhomboid. Use the tangram below to construct your own shapes, pictures and designs.

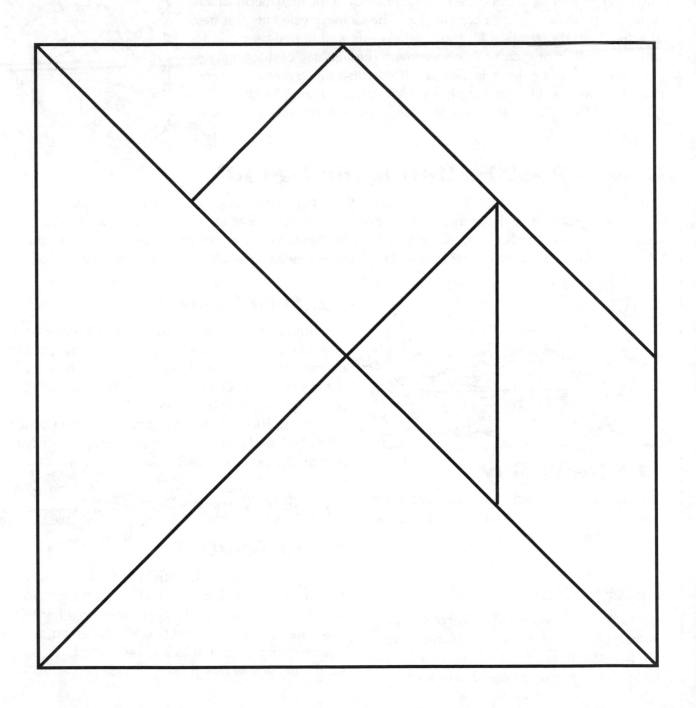

Chinese Dragon

Everybody knows about the Chinese dragon! Here's a game that all your students will love. First, have your students form a single-file line. Then have your students put their hands around the waist of the person in front of them. Have the last person in line tuck a handkerchief into the back of their pants or belt. Then when you blow the whistle, the head of the dragon (the first person in line) tries to catch its tail (the handkerchief on the back of the last person in line). What's fun about this game is that the first few people in line know what to do, they're chasing after the tail. And the last few people know what to do too, they're staying away from the head. But those players in the middle, well, they're not sure whether to go after the tail or stay away from the head. When the head finally does catch the tail, then the head becomes the new tail and the second person in line becomes the new head of the dragon. Have fun!

27

Chinese Dragon Masks

Here's an art activity relating to the Chinese Dragon game. The dragon is considered to be a lucky symbol in China. Dragons are thought to be responsible for gift giving, bringing rain and keeping peace. During the Chinese New Year's celebration, dragons are part of the parades and dances. Some dragons are as long as one mile!

To make a Chinese dragon that is slightly less than a mile long, you will need the Chinese Dragon Patterns reproducible (page 30); a brown paper bag for each child; white, green, red, yellow and black construction paper; scissors; glue; tape; pencils and a black marker.

Here's what you do. Have your students work with a partner for this first step. Begin by having one student place a paper bag on their head. Ask their partner to gently mark where the eyes and mouth should be placed. Then do the same for the other partner. After removing the paper bag from their heads, have each student cut out two almond-shaped eyes. They can use the pattern on the reproducible for a little help. To make the eyes more dramatic, outline each eye with a black marker.

To add horns to the dragon mask, first have your students cut out the horn pattern from their reproducible. Trace the pattern onto black construction paper. Then glue them in place above the eyes.

Next, your students should cut out the sharp dragon teeth on the reproducible and glue them to a 3" x 8" (8 x 20 cm) piece of red construction paper. To make the teeth more dramatic, outline each tooth with a black marker. The entire mouth can then be glued onto the paper bag.

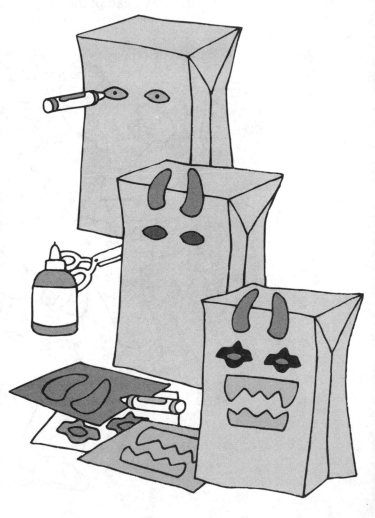

28

For a wicked tongue, cut red construction paper into strips. Make the tip of the tongue forked. Then cut a slit into the dragon's mouth. Fold the end of the tongue and slide it through the slit. Glue the tab on the inside of the paper bag.

Add ferocious-looking nostrils by using a black marker.

To make the dragon's scales, have each student cut a sheet of green construction paper in half lengthwise. Glue the two pieces together to make one long strip. Have your students cut out the dragon scales pattern. Then they can trace the pattern on the green construction paper and fold along the tabs. Now glue the scales along the top of the paper bag and down the side. Your students can also use the scale pattern from the reproducible to make the eyes scarier. Cut the individual scales from the scale pattern and glue them around the eyes.

Finally, cut out the ear pattern from the reproducible. Next, have your students trace the pattern onto yellow construction paper. Fold the bottom edge to create a tab. Then glue the tab to the top of the paper bag.

Your students now have dragon masks for the Chinese Dragon game. You can make your dragon more authentic by stapling an old sheet to the bottom of the paper bag and have your students hide underneath it just as the dragon dancers do in China. You're ready to bring in the new year!

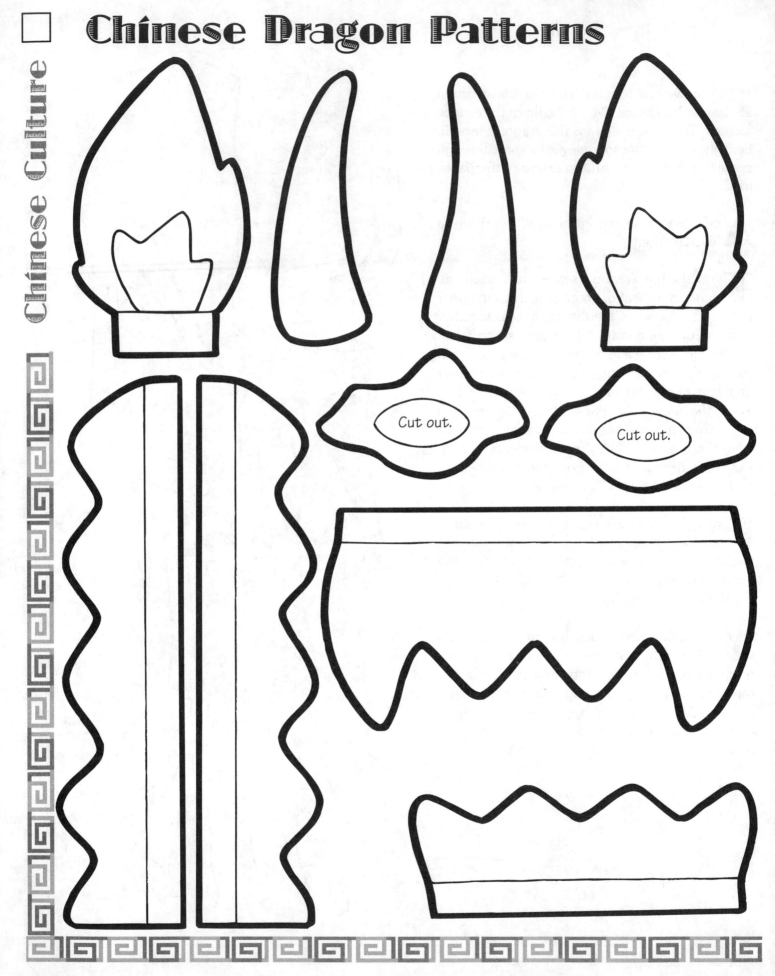

Chinese Dragon Patterns

Chinese Culture

Cut out.

Cut out.

30

Teng Lung (Chinese Lanterns)

Lanterns are carried by families in China for many festivals. During the Lantern Festival, every member of the family carries his own lantern to create a sparkling sea of moving lights. Lanterns are also used in China to decorate store fronts. Your students can create their own lanterns for a mini Lantern Festival.

Materials

Each student will need a 12" x 18" (30 x 46 cm) piece of construction paper, a pipe cleaner, crepe paper streamers, scissors, stapler, pencil and markers.

Procedure

1st: Have your students draw pictures on the 12" x 18" (30 x 46 cm) piece of construction paper; that will be their lantern. You can borrow books on China from your local library, or have students create their own designs.

2nd: Fold the piece of construction paper in half length-wise. Draw a line 1" (2.5 cm) from the edge of the side of the paper opposite the fold. Then, have your students cut slits approximately 1" (2.5 cm) apart from the fold to the line. Open up the paper. Roll with the slits running up and down and staple the ends together.

3rd: To make the handle, punch two holes in the top of the lantern on opposite sides. Bend a pipe cleaner about 1" (2.5 cm) from each end. Then poke the pipe cleaner through the holes and twist it around itself to make a handle. Finally, staple crepe paper streamers to the bottom. Have your students parade around the room!

Chinese New Year's Festival Play

Now that your students have made Chinese dragons and Chinese lanterns for the Chinese New Year, why not have a celebration so that your students can use them? This festival is a great way for your students to display all their hard work for their parents!

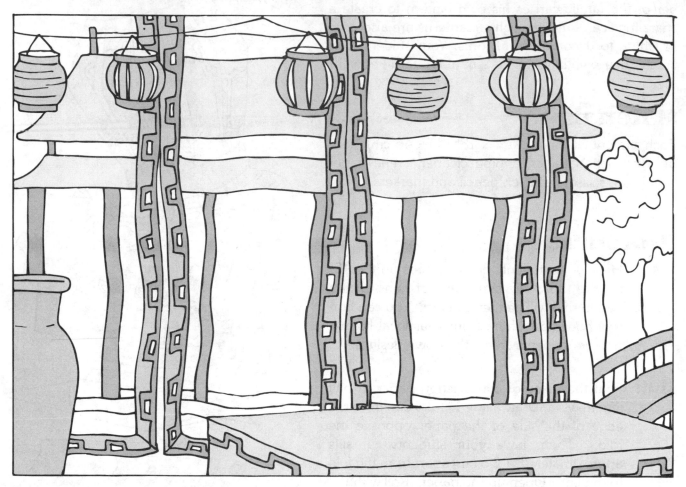

In China, each year is represented by one of 12 animals. Each animal in turn represents a positive personality characteristic that is believed to be shared by all people born in those years. Let your students use the chart provided to familiarize themselves with the animals and to see what animal corresponds to the year that they were born. They can also have some fun finding out the years of their parents', grandparents', brothers', sisters', friends' or relatives' birthdays and determining the matching animal. They might have fun hearing what animal represents the year that you were born!

To produce the Chinese New Year's Festival Celebration Play, use the script that we have provided. You will need a narrator, 12 calendar animals, a dragon and several lantern dancers. If you can find Chinese music, play it! This will add to the flavor of your festival. If your students are really into doing this play, you may also want to make costumes, cards or posters for each calendar animal.

Chinese New Year's Festival Play
SCRIPT

Begin the play with colorful Chinese music!

Narrator: Happy New Year! Listen to that beautiful music! The Chinese New Year Festival is here again! Look! Look! Our New Year celebration is starting with a festival parade, lead by a Chinese dragon. The dragon is sure to bring our class good luck!

The mighty Chinese dragon weaves through the room.

Narrator: Look at those lanterns! The Festival of Lanterns must be beginning!

Students carrying lanterns weave through the room.

Narrator: And now for the highlight of the parade . . . the Chinese calendar animals!

Each animal enters the room in turn.

Dragon: I am the Year of the Dragon. My years are 1964, 1976, 1988 and 2000. I represent courage.

Snake: I am the Year of the Snake. My years are 1965, 1977, 1989 and 2001. I represent wisdom.

Horse: I am the Year of the Horse. My years are 1966, 1978, 1990 and 2002. I stand for cheerfulness.

Ram: I am the Year of the Ram. My years are 1967, 1979, 1991 and 2003. I stand for creativeness.

Monkey: I am the Year of the Monkey. My years are 1968, 1980, 1992 and 2004. I represent good judgement.

Rooster: I am the Year of the Rooster. My years are 1969, 1981, 1993 and 2005. I represent strong belief.

Dog: I am the Year of the Dog. My years are 1970, 1982, 1994 and 2006. If you were born during my year, you are honest.

Pig: I am the Year of the Pig. My years are 1971, 1983, 1995 and 2007. If you were born during my year, you are brave.

Rat: I am the Year of the Rat. My years are 1972, 1984, 1996 and 2008. If you were born during my year, you are ambitious.

Ox: I am the Year of the Ox. My years are 1973, 1985, 1997 and 2009. If you were born during my year, you have patience.

Tiger: I am the Year of the Tiger. My years are 1974, 1986, 1998 and 2010. I represent friendship.

Hare: I am the Year of the Hare. My years are 1975, 1987, 1999 and 2011. I represent good luck.

Narrator: The parade is almost over. Let's take one more look at the New Year's dragon, the Festival of Lanterns and Chinese calendar characters before they leave for another year! Happy New Year!

Students parade around the room one more time.

Chinese Calendar

In China, every year is represented by one of 12 animals. Each animal stands for a positive personality trait. These traits are believed to be shared by all people born in those years. What animal are you? What about your parents, grandparents, brothers, sisters or friends? What animal is your teacher?

Dragon
1964, 1976, 1988, 2000
Courage

Dog
1970, 1982, 1994, 2006
Honesty

Snake
1965, 1977, 1989, 2001
Wisdom

Pig
1971, 1983, 1995, 2007
Bravery

Horse
1966, 1978, 1990, 2002
Cheerfulness

Rat
1972, 1984, 1996, 2008
Ambitious

Ram
1967, 1979, 1991, 2003
Creativeness

Ox
1973, 1985, 1997, 2009
Patience

Monkey
1968, 1980, 1992, 2004
Good Judgement

Tiger
1974, 1986, 1998, 2010
Friendship

Rooster
1969, 1981, 1993, 2005
Strong Belief

Hare
1975, 1987, 1999, 2011
Good Luck

Egg Painting

Chinese egg painting is an ancient tradition that is still practiced today. Very special painted eggs are currently on display in many Chinese temples and holy buildings.

Materials

One egg and one milk bottle cap for each student, paper clips, glue, pencils, watercolor paints, paintbrushes and several small bowls.

Procedure

1st: Hand out one egg and paper clip to each student. Have each student open up the paper clip so that one of its ends is pointing outward. Then using the pointed end of the paper clip, have your students gently tap a small hole in wide end of the egg. The wide end should be facing upward. Try not to crack the whole egg.

2nd: Have your students empty the insides of the egg into the small bowls. Then dry the outside of the eggshell. You might want to save the contents and cook them later. Try the Chinese dish drop egg soup.

3rd: Take the eggshell and glue it placing the broken or wide end onto an inverted milk bottle cap.

4th: Invite your students to gently draw a design on the surface of the eggshell with their pencils.

5th: Using the watercolors and a fine paintbrush, have your students paint their eggshells.

Fun with Fortune Cookies

Everyone likes to break open fortune cookies to reveal their fortune. Here's a fabulous way to use food to get your students to write about their lives. This activity is designed to encourage your students to analyze how the fortune applies to their lives and write a related story on a Chinese scroll.

China has a long history of writing. There is evidence of writing on bones and tortoise shells from 3,500 years ago! As you can imagine, writing on bones and tortoise shells is not the easiest or most convenient of method. In 105 A.D., a frustrated man named Ts'ai Lun decided to find an alternative for the wood and silk used at the time. He mixed a batch of tree bark, plant fibers, hemp, old rags and fishing nets to invent paper. This paper was then attached to wooden sticks to make scrolls. Keep reading to find out how your students can create scrolls that contain stories based on their fortunes.

Here's how you can prepare. If possible, ask a local Chinese resturant or grocery store to donate enough cookies for the students in your class. If you are not able to find the cookies, no problem! We've included fortunes that we have collected so that you can cut them out for your class. If you're feeling super-ambitious, then you can make your own cookies using the recipe provided. In addition to the fortune cookies, your class will need two dowels or sticks, 14" (36 cm) long, per student; 9" x 24" (23 x 61 cm) newsprint or drawing paper; 9" x 24" (23 x 61 cm) rice paper or drawing paper; string or ribbon; pencils; indelible markers; watercolor paints; brushes; glue; ruler and masking tape.

1. First, distribute the fortune cookies or fortunes. Ask students to read their fortunes and decide how it applies or could apply to their life. Allow 15-20 minutes for writing a story about the fortune and their life. You can extend this activity by discussing how the fortune could apply to anyone.

2. Next, have your students draw simple illustrations in pencil that correspond to their story. This works best if the newsprint or drawing paper is oriented hortizontally. They can divide their story into sequential pictures if appropiate. They will also need to rule off 1" (2.5 cm) margins on the sides and 2" (5 cm) margins on the bottom.

3. Now your students are ready to transfer their drawings to the rice paper. They can do so by taping the rice paper on top of their original sketches, then tracing their designs with indelible markers. They can add details and texture to enhance their drawing.

4. With the sketch still taped underneath, use the watercolors to paint over the drawings. Warn your students that the watercolors will bleed on this kind of paper! Allow the paint to dry and remove the tape from the rice paper.

5. Underneath each picture or along the length of the bottom margin, have your students copy their stories about their fortunes and their lives. They might want to glue their original fortune to the paper.

6. Now for the dowels. Apply the glue along the 1" (2.5 cm) margin on each side of the paper. Align the top of the dowel with the top of the paper. Press and roll the dowels into the glue. Make sure the paper wraps all the way around the dowel.

7. Finally, roll up the scroll and secure it with the string or yarn. Your students can then share their fortunes and their stories with the class. If you're really ambitious, have your students present their scrolls at a Chinese food party. Serve Chinese food and try using chopsticks!

38

Fun with Fortunes

If you cannot get fortune cookies for your class, here are some great substitutes! Just cut out the fortunes for each student in your class.

You will make a difference.	Your hard work is about to pay off.
The time is right to make new friends.	Accept the next offer you hear.
Your family brings you much happiness.	You will inherit a lot of money.
Your most memorable dream will come true.	Happiness begins with facing life with a smile and a wink.
Do not listen to those who are critical of your dreams.	You will soon travel long distances.
Many people will request your advice.	You will become rich and famous.
Your have many talents.	You will soon be offered a large reward.
You will soon receive a great honor.	Look for the small joys in life.
Always help others.	All your questions can be answered from within.
Avoid fights; use words instead.	Make music that contains joy.
A friend is smiling because of a good deed you did.	Apologize to someone you hurt. It will bring peace.
You will soon learn a secret.	You will soon learn about other people.

Fortune Cookie Recipe

This recipe is fun to make. It should yield about 30 cookies.

four egg whites

4 egg whites
$1/2$ cup (120 ml) flour
1 cup (240 ml) sugar
$1/4$ teaspoon (1.25 ml) salt
$1/2$ cup (120 ml) melted butter
$1/2$ teaspoon (2.5 ml) vanilla
2 tablespoons (30 ml) water

Blend sugar and egg whites

Melt butter.

1. Preheat oven 375°F (190°C).

2. In a medium-sized bowl, blend the sugar into egg whites until fluffy.

Add flour, salt, vanilla, water and butter.

3. In another bowl, melt the butter, then set aside it aside to cool.

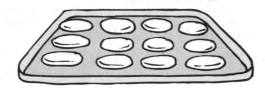

4. Add flour, salt, vanilla, water and butter to the sugar mixture and beat until smooth.

5. Pour the batter in 3" (8 cm) circles onto a well-greased cookie sheet.

6. Bake for 8-10 minutes until golden brown.

7. Lay the fortunes in the center of the cookie. Fold the cookie into thirds, then bend the center gently. (If the cookie gets too hard to bend, reheat it in the oven for a minute or so.)

fortune

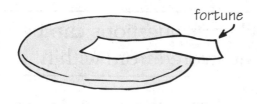

8. Let the cookie cool and harden. Munch away!

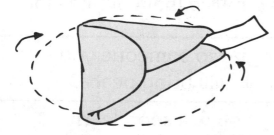

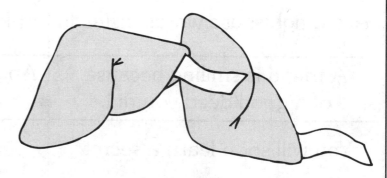

Japanese Culture

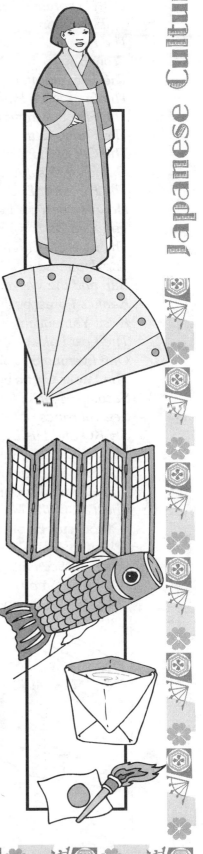

When you think of Japan, do you think of bustling metropolises like Tokyo or tiny rural villages? If you envision both, your perceptions are correct! Many Japanese people who live in a city dwell in a home that has Western-style rooms. Because of the lack of space, they have to live in small apartments that are comparable to apartments found in the United States. In the small villages, or buraku, farming is the main way of life. About one-fourth of the country's population lives in these villages.

In Japan, a unique blend of ancient traditions and past values coexist with modern ideas and ways of life. This contrast between traditional and modern is a defining feature of Japanese society today. Due to Japan's recent economic growth and development as the leading industrial nation in Asia, Japanese people must deal with the problems all city-dwellers encounter. Changes in the traditional Japanese way of life are a result of growing cities, industry and transportation and communication networks. Yet religion, politics and family are still important in Japanese society. Respect for the past, personal loyalty and obligations to family continue to be prized.

Japanese people began to immigrate to the United States in the 1860s. A steady stream of Japanese laborers and students were welcomed to their new home. Japanese Americans usually lived in their own colonies, and worked for lumber camps, railroad companies, fisheries, small factories, on farms or started their own small businesses. Many remained in the United States, even though naturalization privileges were denied. In the early 1900s, just as the Japanese began to become settled on the West Coast an anti-Japanese movement began lead by labor leaders, newspapers and politicians. Many Japanese people were forced to live segregated in social isolation. Laws were passed that hindered Japanese Americans from enjoying all of the rights and benefits of citizens and prevented more Japanese immigrants from arriving. Immigration decreased, yet discrimination against the Japanese continued. These discriminatory laws were repealed, yet Japanese Americans continued to face racism in subsequent years.

During World War II, Japanese Americans on the West Coast were racially segregated after the attack on Pearl Harbor in 1941. Japanese Americans were forced to leave their homes and enter confinement camps. Over 110,000 Japanese Americans lost their homes, jobs and property. Since World War II, Japanese Americans have fought against negative stereotypes and racism. By sharing this group's struggle for citizenship and acceptance in the United States, your students will become more sensitive to Japanese Americans and other immigrants coming to this country today who share the same challenges.

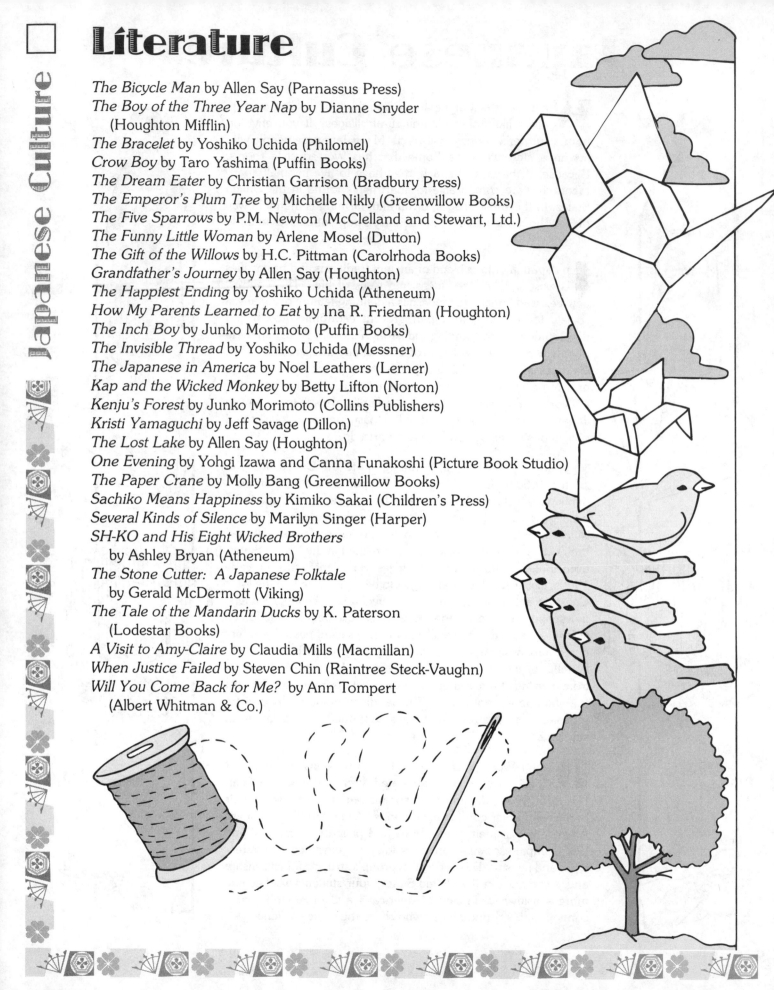

Literature

The Bicycle Man by Allen Say (Parnassus Press)

The Boy of the Three Year Nap by Dianne Snyder
    (Houghton Mifflin)

The Bracelet by Yoshiko Uchida (Philomel)

Crow Boy by Taro Yashima (Puffin Books)

The Dream Eater by Christian Garrison (Bradbury Press)

The Emperor's Plum Tree by Michelle Nikly (Greenwillow Books)

The Five Sparrows by P.M. Newton (McClelland and Stewart, Ltd.)

The Funny Little Woman by Arlene Mosel (Dutton)

The Gift of the Willows by H.C. Pittman (Carolrhoda Books)

Grandfather's Journey by Allen Say (Houghton)

The Happiest Ending by Yoshiko Uchida (Atheneum)

How My Parents Learned to Eat by Ina R. Friedman (Houghton)

The Inch Boy by Junko Morimoto (Puffin Books)

The Invisible Thread by Yoshiko Uchida (Messner)

The Japanese in America by Noel Leathers (Lerner)

Kap and the Wicked Monkey by Betty Lifton (Norton)

Kenju's Forest by Junko Morimoto (Collins Publishers)

Kristi Yamaguchi by Jeff Savage (Dillon)

The Lost Lake by Allen Say (Houghton)

One Evening by Yohgi Izawa and Canna Funakoshi (Picture Book Studio)

The Paper Crane by Molly Bang (Greenwillow Books)

Sachiko Means Happiness by Kimiko Sakai (Children's Press)

Several Kinds of Silence by Marilyn Singer (Harper)

SH-KO and His Eight Wicked Brothers
    by Ashley Bryan (Atheneum)

The Stone Cutter: A Japanese Folktale
    by Gerald McDermott (Viking)

The Tale of the Mandarin Ducks by K. Paterson
    (Lodestar Books)

A Visit to Amy-Claire by Claudia Mills (Macmillan)

When Justice Failed by Steven Chin (Raintree Steck-Vaughn)

Will You Come Back for Me? by Ann Tompert
    (Albert Whitman & Co.)

Celebrations

O-Bon

Imagine thousands of floating candles shimmering on the water during the Feast of Lanterns. This beautiful sight is just one part of this happy holiday. The lanterns are lit in memory of those who have died, special foods are prepared and Buddhist priests lead Bon dances at the temples. This holiday is also a deeply religious holiday celebrated since the introduction of Buddhism in Japan about 1300 years ago. On this day, Japanese people believe that the living reunite with the spirits of the dead.

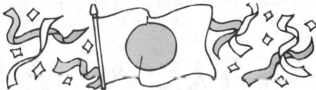

National Foundation Day

On February 11 the founding of Japan in 660 B.C. is celebrated.

Vernal Equinox Day

On the first day of spring, the appreciation of nature and living things is expressed.

New Year's Day (Shoogatsu)

For the Japanese, New Year's Day is a very important celebration. This three-day holiday starts on January 1 with families cleaning their houses. The gateways of most houses, shrines and temples are decorated with rice-straw ropes and pine branches. The ropes are thought to bring good luck and keep away evil and the branches symbolize long life and virtue. People visit shrines, temples, relatives and friends.

Coming of Age Day

On January 15 a ceremony is held for those children that reach the legal age.

Greenery Day

On April 29 plant life in Japan is honored. This holiday which was started in 1989 is the result of former Emperor Hirohito's intense interest in plants.

Constitution Memorial Day

On May 3 the signing of the constitution in 1947 is commemorated.

Celebrations

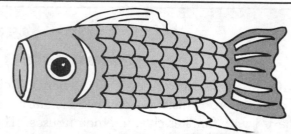

Children's Day

On May 5 hope is expressed that each child will grow up to be brave, strong and healthy. A large carp kite is flown from a long bamboo pole in front on every house. Carp are strong fish that have to fight their way up stream against strong currents.

Respect for the Aged Day

On September 15 the elderly, who have spent their lives dedicated to society, are respected and honored. On this holiday the elderly are given gifts and entertained.

Culture Day

On November 3 love, freedom and Japanese culture is honored.

Autumnal Equinox Day

On the first day of fall, all ancestors are honored.

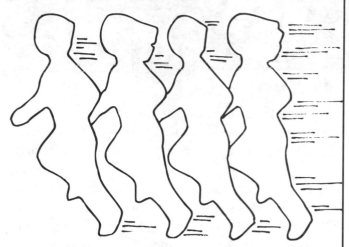

Health-Sports Day

On October 10 the 1964 Tokyo Olympics is commemorated. The purpose of this national holiday is to inspire people to build a sound mind and a healthy body.

Emperor's Birthday

On December 24 the people of Japan honor the Emperor and Empress.

44

Puure Booru! Play Ball!

Puure booru!

What do you think is the most popular sport in Japan? You guessed it . . . baseball! The Tokyo Giants are Japan's most popular baseball team. They're so popular that they have almost single-handedly made baseball the most important sport in Japan. So, what do you think would be a good Japanese game to play with your students? Baseball, Japanese style! Is baseball played differently in Japan? Well, of course it is! You don't think the umpire yells, "Striiiike!" do you? The umpire yells, "Sturiki!" Here are some other common Japanese baseball terms you and your class will want to use when they go out to the playground to "Puure booru." (By the way, in case you haven't guessed it, *Puure booru* means "play ball.")

hitto = hit
sturiki = strike
fouru = foul
booru = ball
puure = play

Furoshiki Mawaski
(Scarf Passing Game)

Japanese people take great care in most everything they do, even when wrapping presents! No sloppily taped corners here. If your students give you a beautifully wrapped gift, then you know that they respect you! (Well, at least if you lived in Japan.) Japanese people wrap presents with both paper and a special cloth called a furoshiki. Those of you who are envirnomentalists will like the idea of a furoshiki, since it can be used later to carry things like books or lunches to school.

Here's another way to use a furoshiki. For this game, you'll need at least one scarf for every three to four players. In addition, you may want to play music, although it is not necessary. First, organize your students so that they are standing in a circle facing the center. Then distribute a scarf to every third or fourth player in the circle. Players holding the furoshikis must tie it around their neck, nod three times, then untie the scarf and pass it to the next player on their right. That player should also tie it around their neck, nod three times before passing it on. And subsequent players should also do the same. Players beware . . . if a player is caught with two scarves, they're out! The last two players left in the game are the winners. Who do you think will be the fastest scarf passer?

Tanko Bushi

We're pretty sure that people in Japan were performing this dance before Beavis and Butthead's version on MTV. No need to worry, this dance is completely appropiate for your classroom, but chances are someone will already know this dance from the popular TV show. If they do, encourage them to lead the class in this original Japanese version!

You too can perform the best-known traditional dance in Japan right in your room. Tanko Bushi basically means the "coal miner's" dance. It is performed by actually pantomining the actions of coal mining.

If you would like to include music, any song with a 4/4 beat will do. First, form your students into a circle facing counterclockwise. Your students will be happy to hear that no partners are needed! The first 16 counts are the Introduction. The dancers simply wait in place. The first action that the dancers pantomime is digging coal. Your students should pretend to hold a shovel with both hands. For two counts, the dancers lift the shovel up while lifting their right foot to their left knee. As they touch their right foot back to the floor, they simultaneously thrust their shovel downward. Repeat this action for two counts. Then your students should face to the left and repeat the action digging and stepping with their left foot. Whew! Anyone sweating yet from all of that hard work? Now your students are ready to throw the coal. As they touch their right heel forward, they throw the coal over their shoulder still using the pretend shovel. On the second count of this action, they lower their right toe to the floor. For the next two counts they repeat this step with their left foot and their left shoulder. Step back! You don't want to get hit by any coal! The entire dance takes 28 counts and can be repeated as many times as you desire.

Sensu

Beautiful sensu, or Japanese fans, seem to have always been a part of the Japanese culture. Wouldn't you like to have a sensu to cool you down on a hot day? Originally, that's what these fans were used for. Later, fans were incorporated into traditional dances. Today, sensu are used for both dances and decoration. The designs on the fans are typically landscapes, outdoor scenes, birds, flowers or even poems. To make your own sensu, use crayons or watercolors to complete the fan below. Then start from the bottom of the page and fold the paper "accordion-style" back and forth. Finally, staple the bottom of the folds together. Use your fan to cool off on a hot day! Or dance, dance, dance!

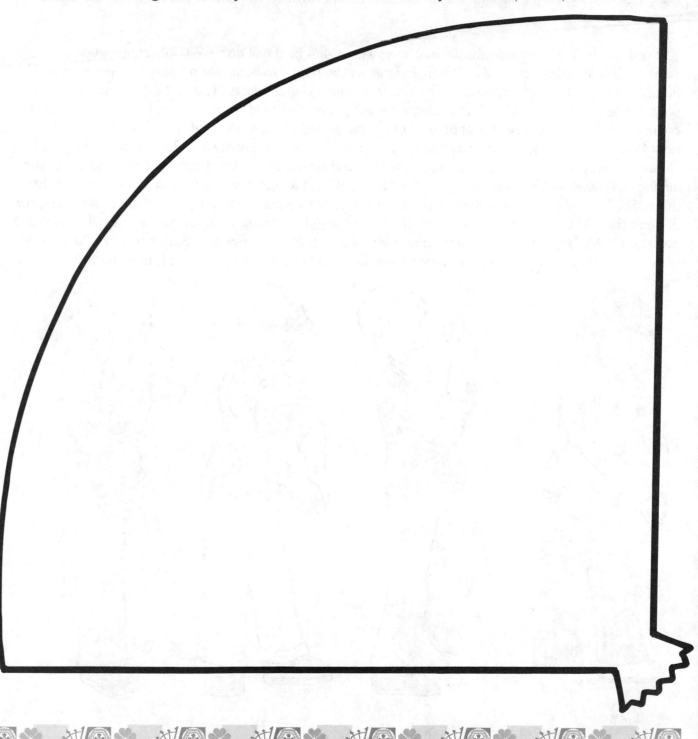

Fantastic Folding Screens

Japanese artists are known around the world for their beautiful folding screens made of hand-carved wood and hand-painted silk panels. These artists usually choose landscapes or flowers as their subject matter.

Materials

Your students can replicate these screens using the Fantastic Folding Screens reproducible (page 50), tissue paper, tape, markers and scissors.

Procedure

1st: To begin making a miniature folding screen, have your students fold their reproducible in half along the dotted line.

2nd: Then fold each half backwards to the fold. Repeat this step for both sides.

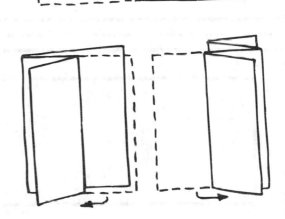

3rd: Now, have your students cut out the shapes on each panel of the screen. They will also need to cut out pieces of tissue paper that are slightly bigger than the openings. Tape the pieces of tissue paper to the back of the screen to imitate silk.

4th: Finally, have your students draw landscapes and flowers on the bottom of the screens. Once completed, have your students stand the screens upright and admire their works of beauty!

tissue

Fantastic Folding Screens

Cut out.

Cut out.

Cut out.

Cut out.

Origami Drinking Cup

Japanese children begin to learn simple paper folding in kindergarten. Origami enhances fine motor skills and develops creative abilities. Later, Japanese children learn how to fold paper to create animals, houses, birds, people and boats, among other things!

Materials

To begin your class' folding paper frenzy, pass out sheets of 8" (20 cm) origami paper or 8½" x 11" (22 x 28 cm) typing paper. If your class is using 8½" x 11" (22 x 28 cm) paper, instruct them to fold the bottom corner on a diagonal, aligning it with the perpendicular edge. By cutting off the excess paper at the top, your students will begin with the traditional square.

Your students are now ready to make a drinking cup that will actually hold water. This activity is perfect right before recess!

Procedure

1st: Take the square paper and fold it on the diagonal. (If your class used the 8½" x 11" [22 x 28 cm] paper, your students have already done this step.)

2nd: Then fold the left corner to the middle of the right edge. Repeat this step with the right corner—fold the right corner to the middle of the left edge.

3rd: Then fold down the triangular flaps at the top of the cup in the opposite direction. To open the cup, squeeze the fold lines gently. Have your students stop at the nearest drinking fountain to take a cool refreshing drink in their functional paper cup!

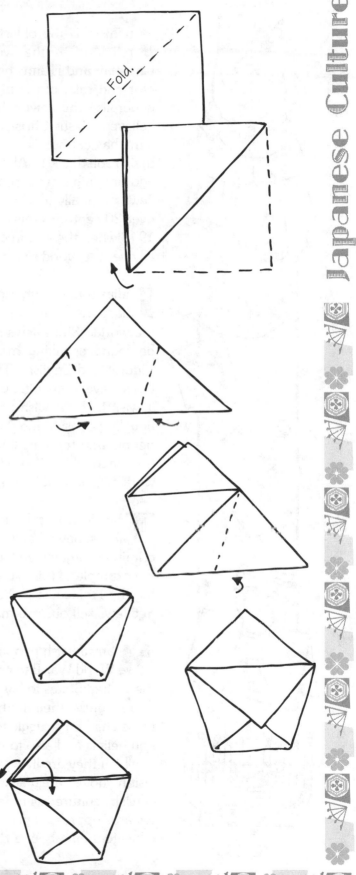

Jewish Culture

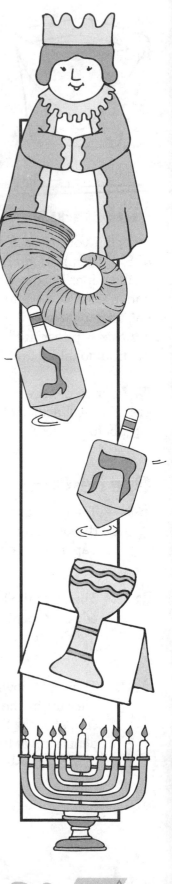

Judaism is the oldest of the three major monotheistic religions in the world. Jewish people share the Christian and Islamic belief that one God exists as the creator and ruler of the universe. Although many non-Jews generalize the Jewish faith as the religion that does not believe in Jesus Christ, Judaism is a complex religious system that cannot be so easily characterized. Jews trace their roots back to Abraham, who lived over 3,000 years ago and is believed to be the father of this faith. Ancient Jews originally lived in Palestine in the Middle East. For over 20 centuries this land was ruled by other people until 1948 when the nation of Israel was formed and Jews from all over the world returned to their "homeland."

Judiasm has many rich and varied traditions due to the diaspora, or the spreading of Jewish people throughout the world. Since Jews reside in many countries, they can be found speaking many languages, including Hebrew, Yiddish and English. Throughout history many other cultures have both influenced and been influenced by the Jewish faith. Jewish contributions to the world are mind-boggling considering the relatively small number of Jewish people and the hardships that they have faced. Think of how incredibly different our world would be without the work of Sigmund Freud, Albert Einstein or Beverly Sills!

The Jewish culture contains both sadness and joy. Jews have been systematically oppressed and discriminated against for several millennia. The most horrifying example of this is the massacre of six million Jews during the Holocaust in Nazi Germany during World War II. Yet Jews still observe many wonderful celebrations.

Many Jewish people came to the United States during World War II to escape the Nazis. Jewish children in the United States today live in a society that does not readily recognize their faith, holidays and traditions. Often these children struggle to adhere to their cultural traditions and beliefs and also to fit into the mainly Christian society in which they are living. Schools, shopping malls and television shows rarely acknowledge their faith. Studying the Jewish culture will develop your students' sensitivity towards oppressed people, reduce prejudicial attitudes and educate them about a rich religious culture.

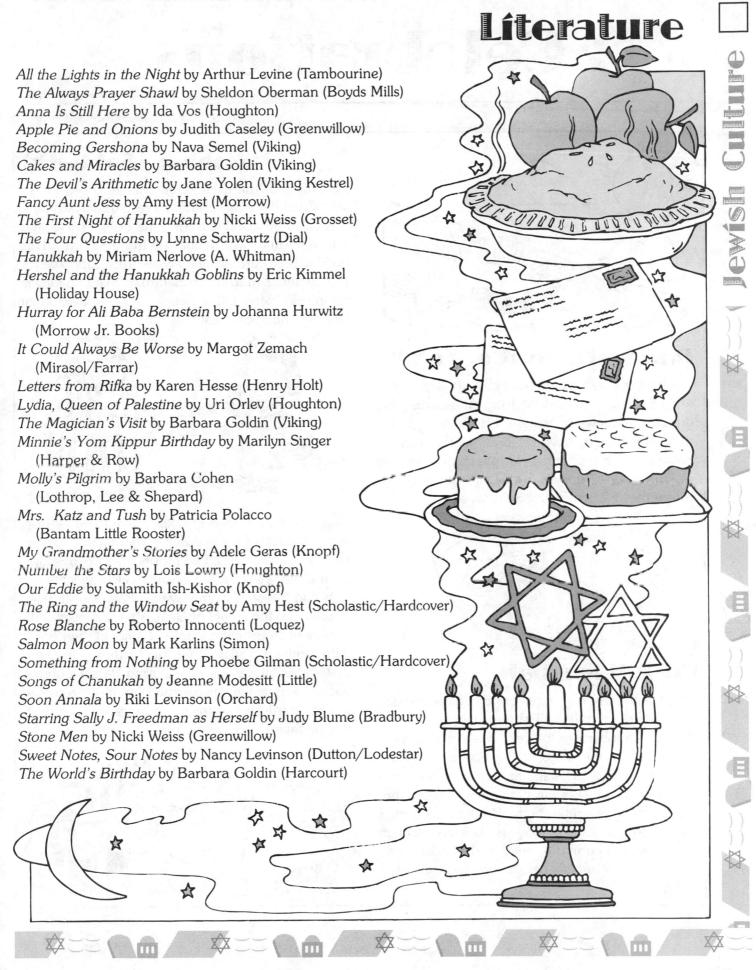

Literature

All the Lights in the Night by Arthur Levine (Tambourine)
The Always Prayer Shawl by Sheldon Oberman (Boyds Mills)
Anna Is Still Here by Ida Vos (Houghton)
Apple Pie and Onions by Judith Caseley (Greenwillow)
Becoming Gershona by Nava Semel (Viking)
Cakes and Miracles by Barbara Goldin (Viking)
The Devil's Arithmetic by Jane Yolen (Viking Kestrel)
Fancy Aunt Jess by Amy Hest (Morrow)
The First Night of Hanukkah by Nicki Weiss (Grosset)
The Four Questions by Lynne Schwartz (Dial)
Hanukkah by Miriam Nerlove (A. Whitman)
Hershel and the Hanukkah Goblins by Eric Kimmel
    (Holiday House)
Hurray for Ali Baba Bernstein by Johanna Hurwitz
    (Morrow Jr. Books)
It Could Always Be Worse by Margot Zemach
    (Mirasol/Farrar)
Letters from Rifka by Karen Hesse (Henry Holt)
Lydia, Queen of Palestine by Uri Orlev (Houghton)
The Magician's Visit by Barbara Goldin (Viking)
Minnie's Yom Kippur Birthday by Marilyn Singer
    (Harper & Row)
Molly's Pilgrim by Barbara Cohen
    (Lothrop, Lee & Shepard)
Mrs. Katz and Tush by Patricia Polacco
    (Bantam Little Rooster)
My Grandmother's Stories by Adele Geras (Knopf)
Number the Stars by Lois Lowry (Houghton)
Our Eddie by Sulamith Ish-Kishor (Knopf)
The Ring and the Window Seat by Amy Hest (Scholastic/Hardcover)
Rose Blanche by Roberto Innocenti (Loquez)
Salmon Moon by Mark Karlins (Simon)
Something from Nothing by Phoebe Gilman (Scholastic/Hardcover)
Songs of Chanukah by Jeanne Modesitt (Little)
Soon Annala by Riki Levinson (Orchard)
Starring Sally J. Freedman as Herself by Judy Blume (Bradbury)
Stone Men by Nicki Weiss (Greenwillow)
Sweet Notes, Sour Notes by Nancy Levinson (Dutton/Lodestar)
The World's Birthday by Barbara Goldin (Harcourt)

Celebrations

Purim (Festival of Lots)

Purim is celebrated between February and March to remember the story of King Ahasuerus who granted the Jews in Israel the right to fight for their lives. Cities have celebrations that include parades, parties, dramatic presentations and masquerades. Puppets are usually made to represent the characters in the Purim story.

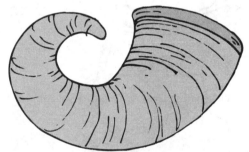

Rosh Hashanah

The Jewish New Year is celebrated on the first day of the Jewish month of Tishri, usually in the middle of September or October. Rosh Hashanah is celebrated for two days at the beginning of the High Holy Days. The shofar, or ram's horn, is a special part of this celebration. Jews believe that their names are written in the Book of Life with a list of their good and bad deeds. During the High Holy Days the book is opened so that people can amend their misdeeds before the Book is closed again.

Shabbat (Sabbath)

According to the Bible, God created the world in six days and on the seventh he rested. Jews imitate this belief by working during the week and resting and reflecting on Shabbat or the Sabbath. This holiday is celebrated every week from sundown on Friday until sundown on Saturday. The holiday is often celebrated with a delicious meal, traditional prayers and special candles.

Passover

This celebration usually takes place in March or April and lasts for eight days. Symbolic of when the Jewish people, led by Moses, fled Egypt more than 3,000 years ago, Passover celebrates liberation and freedom from slavery. Passover literally means that the Angel of Death "passed over" the homes of all Israelites who had marked their door with lamb's blood so that the firstborn of every Jewish family was saved. During Passover Jews eat matzoh–a flat, unleavened bread–to remember the hardships of their ancestors in the desert during their exodus from Egypt.

TLC10012 Copyright © Teaching & Learning Company, Carthage, IL 62321

Celebrations

Yom Kippur

Yom Kippur, or the "Day of Atonement," is the tenth day of Rosh Hashanah. Yom Kippur is a solemn time for Jewish people to reflect on their sins and failings and to have a chance at a new beginning. People attend prayer services and fast on this day as a way to symbolize the cleansing of the soul.

Sukkot (Harvest Festival)

For a week in late September or October a festival celebrating the harvest is observed by building a small kiosk in the backyard. These represent the tents that Jewish people lived in thousands of years ago during harvest time to more efficiently harvest their crops. They also represent the tents that the Jews used during their exodus from Egypt. During the Sukkot, family members may eat, study and sleep in the kiosk. Food is also distributed to families in need.

Hanukkah

Every December the Feast of Lights is celebrated. This holiday celebrates the miracle of a lamp burning for eight days when it only had enough fuel to burn for one day. This miracle happened 2,000 years ago when the Jewish people won back their right to practice their own religion. Hanukkah is a feast celebrating freedom. The menorah, a special nine-branch candelabra, is lit during this celebration.

Dreidel Game

This game is usually played during Hanukkah, but in the times when Jews were forbidden to practice their religion, they would meet to play dreidel games while secretly praying. A dreidel is a four-sided top with the Hebrew letters *nun, gimmel, hay* and *shin,* written on each side. When combined, the letters on the dreidel stand for "Nes gadol hayoh sham" or "A Great Miracle Happened Here." This game helps children to remember the miracle of the eight-day burning lamp of Hanukkah.

Reproduce the dreidel pattern on page 57 for each pair of students playing. Directions for making the dreidel and a lucky dreidel charm are given for the students. You will need to provide the students with crayons or markers, scissors, glue or tape, and string or yarn. Students also need a pencil or a pen.

Dreidel games are usually played with candy, nuts, or raisins. So make sure each player has a pre-determined number of pieces of candy, nuts, or raisins. Players win or lose depending on which letter is up when the top falls. Players should place one piece of candy, nut, or raisin in the kitty before each turn. One player takes a turn spinning the dreidel. When the dreidel lands, the side facing up will dictate what that player will do. Players alternate taking turns. Here are the directions per side of the dreidel:

Gimmel

Hay

Shin

Nun

Gimmel: The player wins the whole kitty.

Hay: The player wins half of the kitty.

Nun: The player does nothing.

Shin: The player must place one piece of candy, nut or raisin in the kitty.

Students can also practice addition while playing with their dreidels. Each letter in the Hebrew alphabet also has a number value:

Gimmel = 3
Hay = 5
Nun = 50
Shin = 300

Have students tally their score after each spin. Highest score wins.

Dreidel Cube and Charm

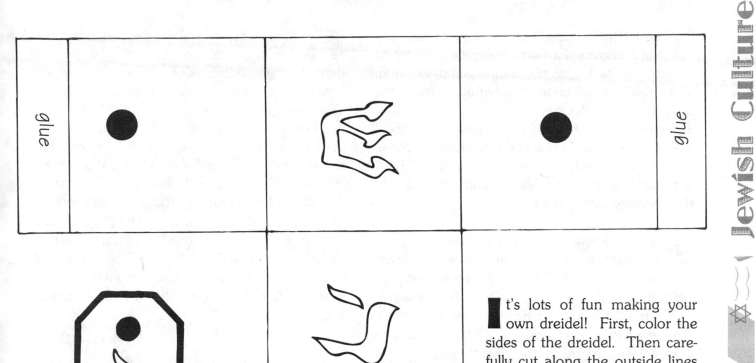

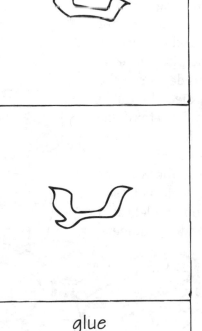

glue

It's lots of fun making your own dreidel! First, color the sides of the dreidel. Then carefully cut along the outside lines of the dreidel pattern. Next, use a pencil point to punch holes where shown. The dreidel is now ready to be folded along the inside lines. Glue or tape along the tabs to form the dreidel into a cube. Finally push a pencil or pen through the holes to finish your dreidel or top.

For a little extra luck, make your own dreidel charm necklace. The lucky dreidel charm always shows the gimmel, the letter that wins the entire kitty. Cut out the lucky dreidel charm; then punch a hole at the top. Color the gimmel your favorite color. Push a piece of string or yarn through the hole and tie the ends together. Slip the necklace over your head. Spin the dreidel to start the game! Good luck!

Lag B'Omer Aim Game

The festival of Lag B'Omer is celebrated during Passover. Farmers brought one omer, or measure of barley, to the temple as an offering. The rabbis would count the barley to mark the days between Passover and Shavuot, another Jewish festival. As you know from the dreidel game, each letter in the Hebrew alphabet corresponds to a number. *Lag* means "thirty-three," therefore *Lag B'Omer* means "Thirty-third day of the counting of the Omer."

Several significant events in Jewish history occurred on Lag B'Omer, hence the reason for celebration. During ancient times, Jews in Palestine lived under the rule of the Romans. When the Jews felt the Roman rule was unjust, they went to war. During one of these wars, a plague killed many of the Jewish soldiers who were also students. On the thirty-third day of Omer, miraculously the plague ceased. In memory of the soldier-students, Lag B'Omer is also called the "Scholar's Holiday."

While Romans dominated, Jews were forbidden to practice their religion. But Rabbi Shimon Bar Yohai ignored the Roman laws and continued to teach Judiasm. When the Romans discovered this, the Rabbi and his son were forced to flee to the countryside. To fool the Romans, students carrying bows, arrows and picnic baskets would venture out to the countryside to see the Rabbi. After the Roman emperor died, the Rabbi and his son returned home on the thirty-third day of Omer or Lag B'Omer. Today, Jewish children all over the world have substituted the bows and arrows the students used to deceive the Romans with the Lag B'Omer Aim Game. Invite your students to test their aim while adding and learning Hebrew letters with their corresponding numbers.

For this game you will need seven empty tuna fish or cat food cans for each group of students playing. Have your students cut strips of construction paper to wrap around all seven cans. Then have your students decorate each strip with the Hebrew letters and symbols. Next, instruct your students to glue the strips to the outside of the seven cans. Then let your students color and cut out each of the Lag B'Omer Aim Game circles provided. Once colored, these circles should be glued to the inside bottom of each can. Finally, have your students arrange the six cans in a circle around the center "double score" can on a piece of cardboard. Have your students glue the cans in place on the cardboard bottom. Now the gameboard is constructed!

Lag B'Omer Aim Game

Cut out the seven game circles below. Follow your teacher's instructions to make your gameboard. To play this game you and your partner are going to need six beans each. Ask your teacher nicely for the beans. Now that you and your partner have your beans, you will take turns throwing all six of your beans, one at a time, into the cans. If you go first, throw all six of your beans into the cans. Remember, each letter in Hebrew also stands for a number. Add up your score with the numbers on the bottom of each can. If you throw a bean in the "double score" can in the middle, make sure you double your score. The highest score wins. Ready-aim-throw!

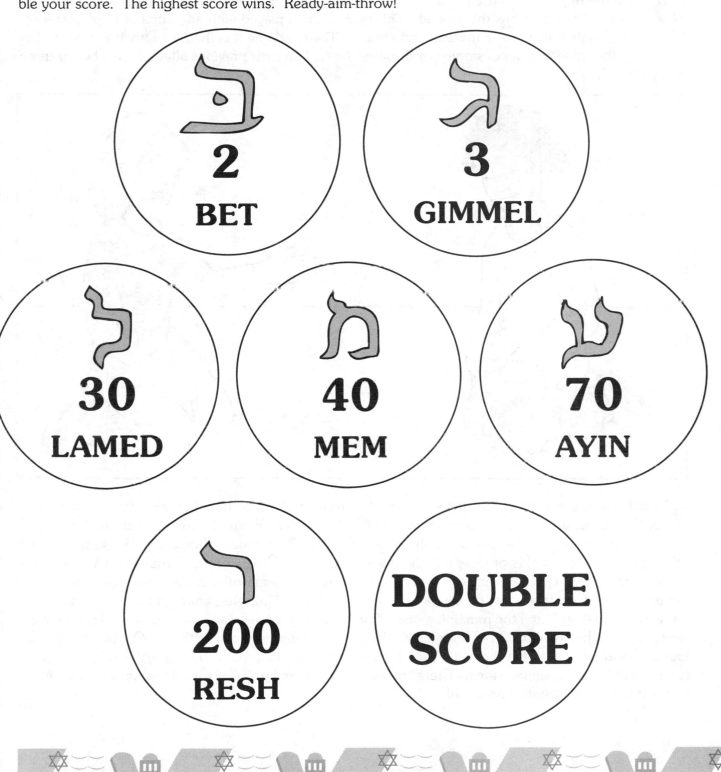

2 BET	**3** GIMMEL
30 LAMED	**40** MEM
70 AYIN	
200 RESH	**DOUBLE SCORE**

Five Stones

For your students who like to play jacks, this game will look very familiar! This game was invented in the rocky parts of Israel. Israel is home to many Jewish children who like to play many of the same games that your students love, including Five Stones or Israeli Jacks. Your students can play using five small stones found in your school yard.

One of the five stones is used as a "ball." Since this "ball" does not bounce, your students will need to catch it before it hits the ground. This game can be played with any number of players, each taking a turn until they make a mistake and are out. The next time it is their turn, they should start by picking up the same number of stones per throw as they did on their previous attempt (one, two or three, etc., per toss).

First, have your students throw the stones on the ground in front of them (just like in jacks). This player then picks up one stone to use as the "ball." The student should throw the "ball" in the air, and with the same hand, pick up one stone then catch the ball. The student should shift the stone into the other hand and repeat this process until he has picked up all of the stones. When students have successfully completed Onesies, they are ready for Twosies. The same rules apply, only when they throw the ball into the air, they must then pick up two stones. For Threesies, your students must sweep up three stones first and then the remaining one. The real pros are now ready for Foursies. Have your students begin with all five stones in their hand. They must dexteriously throw the ball up, place the other four stones down and catch the ball. Then they must pick up four stones first (regular rules apply) followed by the one remaining stone. There are more complicated patterns for this game, which we invite your students to reinvent or research!

In the fifth century B.C., the Jews lived under the rule of the Persians. One evening, Persian King Ahasuerus held a banquet at his palace. King Ahasuerus wanted his wife, Queen Vashti, to show her beauty. Vashti refused, so the King ordered her out of the palace. He then chose a lovely young new queen named Esther. Esther did not tell King Ahasuerus that she was a Jew. She also did not tell the King that her cousin was a man named Mordecai–a Jewish leader.

One day, Mordecai overheard two servants plotting to kill King Ahasuerus. Mordecai warned Esther, and Esther warned the King. The King was very grateful.

A few days later, the King's evil and wicked minister named Haman convinced the King to order all people in his kingdom to bow respectfully before the King. The only man who refused to bow was Mordecai, who only bowed to God. Haman became furious and made plans for Mordecai and all his fellow Jews to be killed. He prepared the gallows for Mordecai and chose the thirteenth day of the twelfth month as the day all Jews would be killed.

That night, the King could not sleep. He asked for the kingdom's records to be read, and by chance the story about Mordecai saving the King's life was read. The King was shocked to find that Mordecai had not recieved special honors. The next day, the King asked Haman how to honor a man who had served the King well. Haman, thinking it was he who was going to be honored, replied that the man should be paraded through the streets in the King's own royal clothing. The King said, "Make haste, do even so to Mordecai the Jew." Haman was horrified that he had to honor Mordecai, his enemy. Haman kept plotting against Mordecai and the Jews.

Again, Mordecai heard of evil Haman's plans and sent word to Esther. Esther planned a banquet for the King and Haman. The King was so pleased by her graciousness that he granted her any wish she desired. Esther boldly stated that she was a Jew and that her people had been condemned to death by Haman. For proof, she told him where the gallows stood for Mordecai and her people. The King was horrified and sentenced Haman to death. The King then gave Esther all of Haman's land and made Mordecai his minister.

By custom, royal decrees could not be reversed. The Jews were still in danger of being killed. Mordecai's first action as minister was to decree that all Jews were allowed to defend themselves on the thirteenth day of the twelfth month. That was the day that Haman had planned to kill the Jews. The Jews fought valiantly against the Persians and won. On the fourteenth day, when the fighting ended, the King and Mordecai proclaimed a holiday, hence Purim.

Purim Finger Puppet Activity

Your students are now ready to produce a Purim Finger Puppet Play. Imagine how excited they will be to write both the script and create the characters' costumes! First, read and discuss the story of Purim. Focus on each character's role. Next, divide the students into groups of four. Provide each group with a copy of the story so they can re-create the character's words. Each student will be responsible for writing and acting the part of one of the characters: King Ahasuerus, Queen Vashti, Queen Esther, Mordecai or Haman. (Since Queen Vashti has a small role, one student can play both Queens.) Using the reproducible provided, the students can continue creating the words of each character. You, or another student, can be the narrator. Once their Purim play is written, they can make their finger puppets. Give each group of four a Purim Finger Puppets page (page 64). Let them cut out each puppet and decorate their character as they wish. Finally, each student can attach a circle of paper that fits around their finger to the back of each puppet. Groups who finish early can create "extras" for their play. The students may want to include other Jews and Persians, servants or a horse. Your class is now ready to produce a first-class play!

You are going to be a playwright, a person who writes plays. First, read and discuss the story of Purim with your class. Now that you know the story of Purim, you are ready to create your very own play!

Decide who is going to be King Ahasuerus, Queen Vashti and Queen Esther, Mordecai and Haman in your group of four. Write your name above your character's name. The story of Purim has been started for you. Read each line of the story carefully. Take turns creating what each character would say. When you are finished, ask your teacher for your Purim Finger Puppets page so you can make the characters come to life!

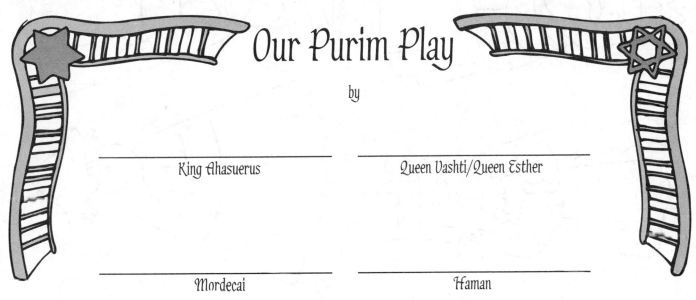

Our Purim Play

by

_____   _____
King Ahasuerus   Queen Vashti/Queen Esther

_____   _____
Mordecai   Haman

Narrator: This is the story of Purim, a Jewish holiday. In the fifth century B.C., the Jews lived under the rule of the Persians. The story begins with King Ahasuerus talking to his wife, Queen Vashti.

King Ahasuerus: I am going to have a banquet at our palace tonight. I want you to show your beauty.

Queen Vashti: No! I do not want to show my beauty!

King Ahasuerus: I am the King, and you must follow my orders. If you choose to disobey, then you must leave the palace.

Narrator: Queen Vashti left the palace as the King's banquet was about to begin.

Purim Finger Puppets

You are now going to be a costume designer. A costume designer is the person who creates what each character will wear. First, cut out your characters below. Next, color and decorate their costumes. Then wrap a strip of paper around your finger. Put one dot of glue between the strips, then glue it to the back of your puppet. Now you're ready to act out your Purim play!

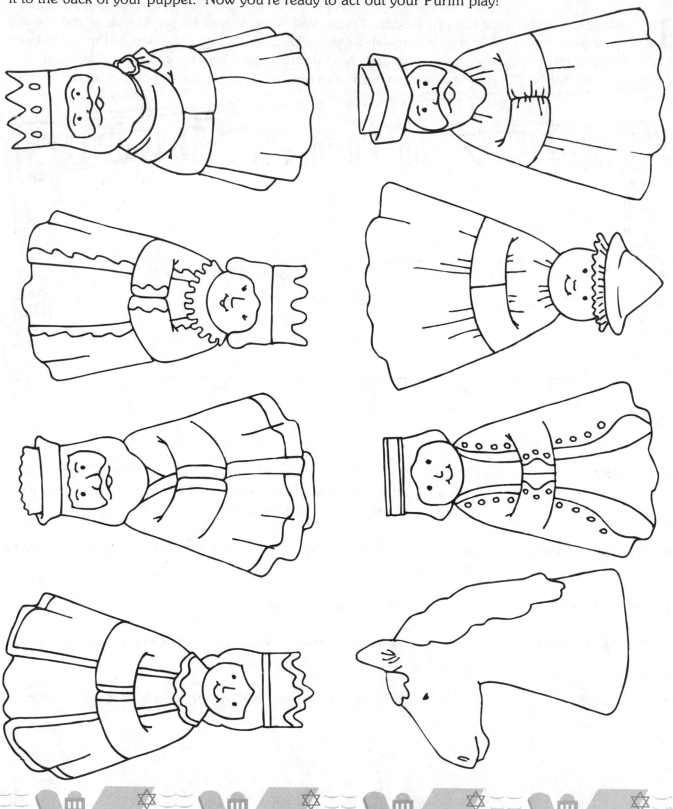

Jewish Calendar

For more than 5,000 years, Jewish people have based their calendar on the moon. Jewish holidays are therefore celebrated on the same day every year of the Jewish lunar calendar. The dates of these holidays change from year to year on the newer Julian calendar, which is based on the sun. Below is a drawing of the two calendars combined. See if you can determine what months these holidays are celebrated in: Martin Luther King's birthday, Valentine's Day, Hanukkah, April Fools' Day, Purim, Fourth of July, Christmas, Passover, Thanksgiving and your birthday.

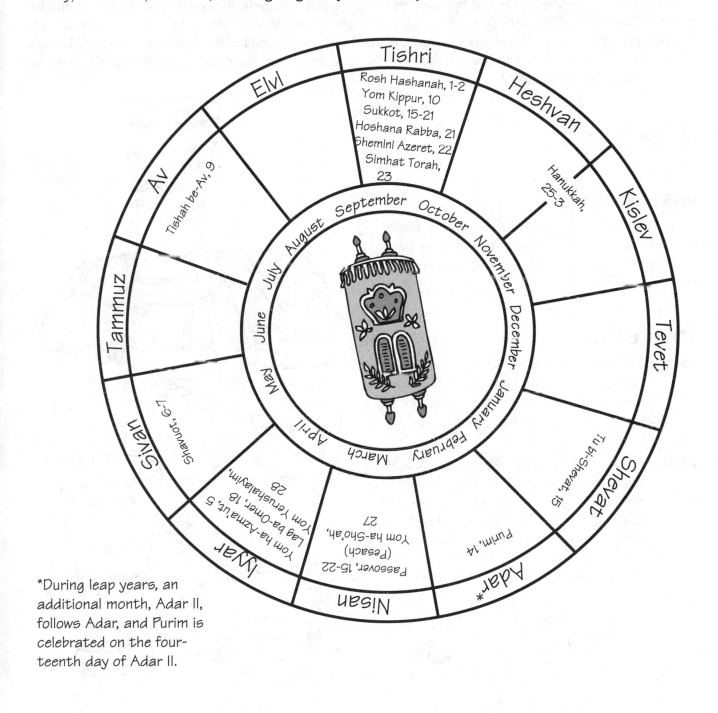

*During leap years, an additional month, Adar II, follows Adar, and Purim is celebrated on the fourteenth day of Adar II.

Seder Cards and Cups

Pesach, or Passover, is one of the most important holidays in the Jewish religion. Passover, or the Festival of Unleavened Bread, celebrates the Jewish peoples' escape from slavery in Egypt. On the first two days of Passover, Jewish people prepare a special meal called a seder, meaning "order." During the meal, certain foods are eaten and prayers are said in a particular order. To explain the historical and religious meaning of the holiday, the Haggadah (from the Hebrew word "to tell") is read. Within the Haggadah, there are stories, prayers, psalms and songs that describe the exodus. The seder is designed to hold children's interest. One of the ways the children participate in the seder is by making a cup for the prophet Elijah. This extra cup is filled with wine and placed in the center of the table. According to legend, during the dinner, Elijah enters every house, sips the wine and heralds the coming of the Messiah. The children look in amazement when they see the wine moving in their cup. Did Elijah really arrive or did someone bump the table?

Goblet

Materials

To make a goblet for the good prophet Elijah, you will need two Styrofoam™ cups (one large and one small for each student), glue and markers.

Procedure

1st: Tell your students to flip over the smaller cup so that it is on the desk upside down. Next, glue the larger cup right side-up onto the bottom of the smaller cup.

2nd: Once the glue dries, have your students decorate their goblets with Passover symbols. They may want to include Elijah's name, the star of David, an Egyptian pyramid, matzoh (unleavened bread) or wine. Your students are now ready to set the table for their seder!

TLC10012 Copyright © Teaching & Learning Company, Carthage, IL 62321

Seder Place Cards

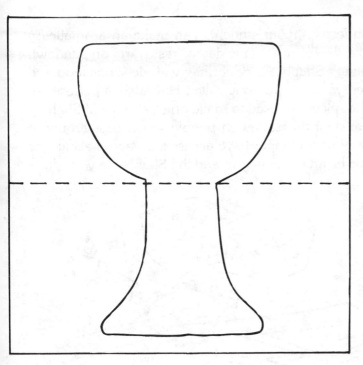

Seder is special feast and a delicious part of Passover, the Jewish Festival of Unleavened Bread. Listen to your teacher's description of the history of Passover and the importance of the seder. Then follow your teacher's directions for making a seder place card and cup of Elijah. When you're finished, you'll be ready to have your own seder dinner!

Materials

Prepare your own seder table setting by making seder place cards and the seder cup of Elijah. To make seder place cards, you are going to need the Seder Place Card reproducible (page 67), scissors, craft knife and crayons or markers. Food for a feast is optional!

Procedure

1st: Color the picture of the cup of Elijah on the reproducible.

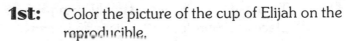

2nd: Next, write your name below the cup. Carefully cut out the top half of the goblet with a craft knife. Make sure that you do not cut out the cup's stem! Then cut out the entire card.

3rd: Finally, fold your place card along the dotted line in the middle of the page. Once the place card is folded, the cup should pop up.

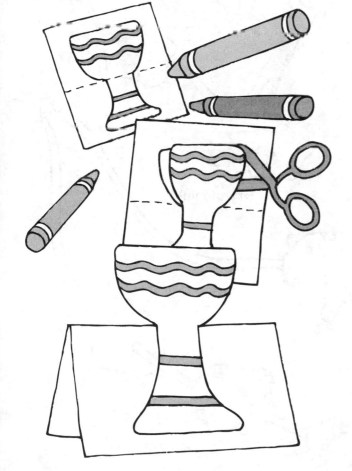

Havdalah Spice Necklaces

To say good-bye to Shabbat and to these Jewish lessons, your students can make an aromatically appealing necklace. Shabbat, or Sabbath, is the day of rest. This day of rest starts on sundown Friday evening and ends on sundown Saturday evening. Shabbat is celebrated with delicious food and rich ceremonies. To bid Shabbat farewell for another week, a ceremony called Havdalah is performed. This ritual uses wine, a braided candle and spices. The spices are used to make one last smell of Shabbat and to carry you through the rest of the week. In ancient times, Jewish people would pass around a sweet-smelling herb from a bush or tree. Since most of us no longer have access to sweet-smelling tree branches, we thought a Havdalah spice necklace would be an easier way to end the Shabbat in your class.

Materials

Your students will need a needle, string or yarn approximately 24" (61 cm) long, spices such as cloves or cinnamon sticks, pieces of recycled Styrofoam™ (here's a great way to reuse the Styrofoam™ trays or "peanuts") and beads (optional).

Procedure

1st: To make the necklace, simply string the pieces of Styrofoam™, spices and beads together.

2nd: Then press the cloves into the pieces of Styrofoam™. If your students have trouble inserting the cloves into the Styrofoam™, they can first make an indentation with their pencil point, and then insert the cloves.

Styrofoam™

3rd: Tie the ends of the strings together. Your students are now ready to don their wearable art!

Korean Culture

The number of Korean immigrants to the United States has increased in recent years. It is therefore important to have a better understanding of the culture of Korea. Korea has a long history with ancient traditions that are changing due to recent industrialization. Like other Asian countries today, urban residents often live and dress with Western influences, while their rural counterparts still retain the traditional way of life. Just as distinctions can be made between the city and the country in Korea, distinctions can be identified between North and South Korea. Although the people in both North and South Korea share the same cultural hertitage, the country has been divided by rival political and economic systems. Since the Korean War, the northern part of the peninsula has been ruled by Communists while the south is non-Communist. In many ways, the country is still trying to recover from this war.

Koreans first came to the United States to work on sugar plantations in Hawaii in 1900. Unlike many other Asian people, Koreans left their country not for the job opportunities in the United States, but rather to escape their country's internal turmoil. Since the 1890s, Korea has been engaged in several brutal wars. Many people fled the country. After Japan took over Korea however, the flow of immigrants to the United States decreased due to Japan's restrictions. Japan did not want Korean immigrants competing with Japanese immigrants for jobs in the United States. Yet, unlike other Asians living in America, Koreans did not want to return to their homeland since it was ruled by a foreign power.

The relatively few Koreans on the West Coast did not provoke as much animosity towards Korean Americans. The anti-Chinese and anti-Japanese sentiments were much stronger. Yet this did not spare Korean Americans from segregation, denied naturalization and restricted immigration laws. Those laws are no longer in effect, but some discriminatory attitudes towards Korean Americans still linger. You can help your students understand the beautiful history, culture and tradition of Koreans and Korean Americans by sharing the following literature, celebrations, games and art activities.

Literature

Aekyung's Dream by Min Paek (Children's Press)

Blindman's Daughter by E.B. Adams and D. Ho Choi (Charles E. Tuttle)

The Buddy Trap by Sheri Sinykin (Atheneum)

Count Your Way Through Korea by James Haskins (Carolrhoda Books)

Families Are Different by Nina Pellegrini (Holiday House)

A Family in South Korea by Swynneth Ashley (Lerner Pub. Co.)

Famous Asian Americans by Janet Morey (Cobblehill/Dutton)

Halmoni and the Picnic by Sook Choi (Houghton)

If It Hadn't Been for Yoon Jun by Marie Lee (Houhton)

The Korean Americans by Brian Lehrer (Chelsea House)

Korean Cinderella by Edward Adams (Seoul International Pub. House)

Koreans by Jodine Mayberry (Watts)

Mail-Order Kid by Joyce McDonald (Putnam)

My Best Friend Mee-Yung Kim by Dianne MacMillan (Messner)

A Pianist's Debut by Barbara Beirne (Carolrhoda Books)

Song Lee in Room 2B by Suzy Kline (Viking)

Soon-Hee in America by Schi-Zhin Rhie (Holym)

Sun and Moon: Fairy Tales from Korea by Kathleen Seros (Holym)

Take a Trip to South Korea by Keith Lye (Franklin Watts, Inc.)

Tuck Triumphant by Theodore Taylor (Doubleday)

We Adopted You, Benjamin Koo by L. Gerard
   (Albert Whitman & Co.)

Celebrations

New Year's Day

On the first day of the first lunar month of the lunar year, Koreans celebrate the New Year. On this day the family dresses in traditional clothes as the memorial ceremony is held in the home. During this ceremony children show respect to their elders by bowing to them and offering good wishes for a long and happy life. Children receive gifts from their elders. The family also plays traditional games at home on this special holiday.

Harvest Moon

This celebration known as Chusok is celebrated on the fifteenth day of the eighth lunar month of the lunar year. This major festival is the Korean Thanksgiving. On this day a memorial service is sometimes performed for deceased ancestors at grave sites. Traditional dances such as the Circle Dance and Farmer's Dance are performed.

Korean Alphabet Day

On October 9 the written alphabet created by decree of the king in 1448 is celebrated.

Tano

In early June, on the fifth day of the fifth lunar month of the lunar year, the full moon night is celebrated. At the family shrine, food for the new summer is offered for deceased ancestors. Many years ago men wrestled on this night, and the winner was awarded the prize of a bull.

National Foundation Day

On October 3 the founding of Korea by Tan-Gun in 2333 B.C. is celebrated.

Full Moon Day

This celebration is observed on the fifteenth day of the first month of the lunar year. On this day of the first full moon of the year, fireworks are lit and many Korean games are played.

Tongji

In December on the longest night of the year Koreans celebrate the winter solstice. Traditionally this celebration was to rid the home of evil spirits.

Yutnori

Yutnori, or Yut, is a popular New Year's Day game which originated in the ninth century during the Paekche dynasty. The game is played by two or four players or teams. For this game, some assembly is required. Traditionally, four wooden sticks called yuts would be used as game pieces. Each yut would have one flat side and one round side. For your class, you can substitute four craft sticks with one side colored black. The wood side is the front, and the black side is the back. Your students will also need one marker for each player or team. You can supply pebbles, beads, buttons or checkers for markers. Finally, photocopy the Yutinori gameboard provided on page 73.

To begin playing, each team or player places their marker on the home space. Players then alternate throwing the four yuts in the air. Each player moves their marker according to how the yuts fall. For:

mah	All four pieces land on their backs. Move five spaces and take an extra turn.
yut	All four pieces land on their fronts. Move four spaces and take an extra turn.
gul	Three pieces show their fronts. Move three spaces.
kae	Two pieces show their fronts. Move two spaces.
toh	One piece shows its front. Move one space.

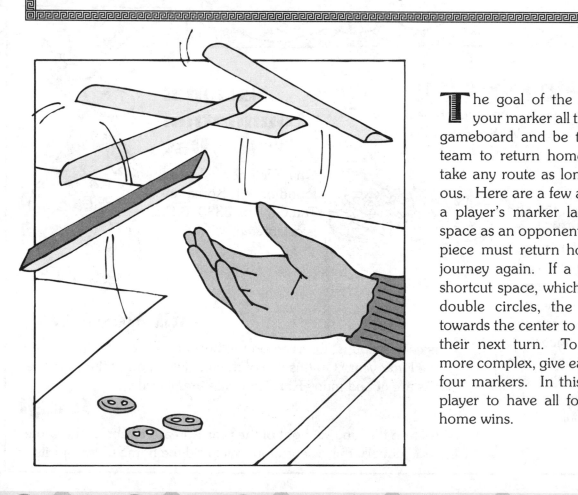

The goal of the game is to move your marker all the way around the gameboard and be the first player or team to return home. A player may take any route as long as it is continuous. Here are a few additional rules: If a player's marker lands on the same space as an opponent's, the opponent's piece must return home to start their journey again. If a player lands on a shortcut space, which is marked by the double circles, the player can turn towards the center to take a shortcut on their next turn. To make this game more complex, give each player or team four markers. In this version, the first player to have all four markers reach home wins.

Yutnori Gameboard

Listen to your teacher's instructions for playing this game. Here is how you keep score:

mah	All four pieces land on their backs. Move five spaces and take an extra turn.
yut	All four pieces land on their fronts. Move four spaces and take an extra turn.
gul	Three pieces show their fronts. Move three spaces.
kae	Two pieces show their fronts. Move two spaces.
toh	One piece shows its front. Move one space.

Good luck!

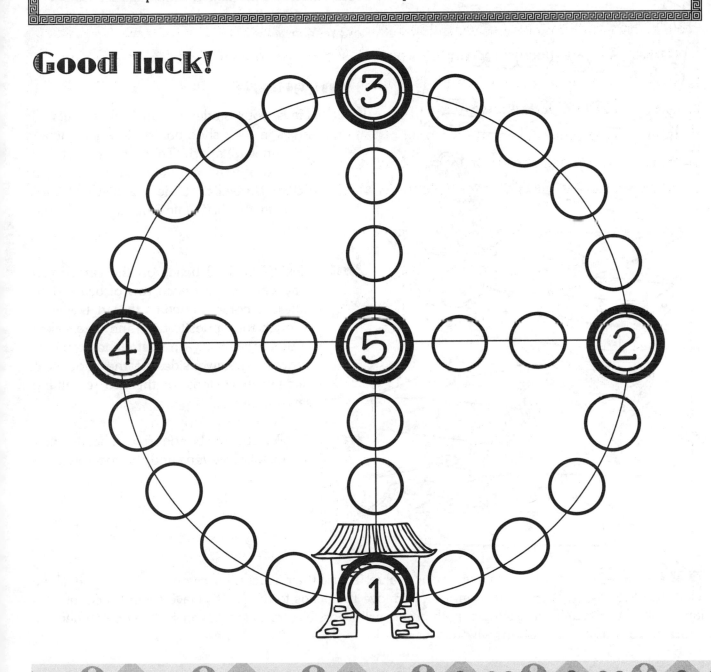

Joo-Pan (Korean Abacus)

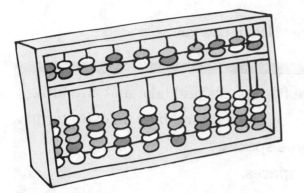

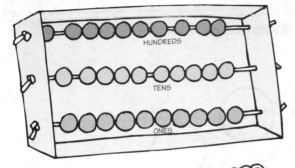

Your students will be surprised to find out that many students in Asian countries use abacuses as quickly and easily as they use calculators. Koreans believe that using an abacus is not only helpful in solving math problems, but it also develops a child's intelligence.

Materials

Your students can make a simplified abacus out of shoe boxes (or lids), beads, yarn, tape, hole punch and marker.

Procedure

1st: Have your students punch three sets of holes in their shoe box or lid a few inches (centimeters) apart. Then knot one end of a piece of yarn and tape the other end to act as a needle. Slide the piece of yarn through the first hole until it reaches the knot.

2nd: Next, thread 10 beads on the yarn. You may want to have each row of beads be a different color. Again, thread the yarn through the opposite hole and tie another knot so that the yarn is stretched taughtly between the two sides of the shoe box. Repeat these steps for the two remaining sets of holes.

3rd: Finally, label the bottom row of beads *ones*, the middle row *tens* and the top row *hundreds*.

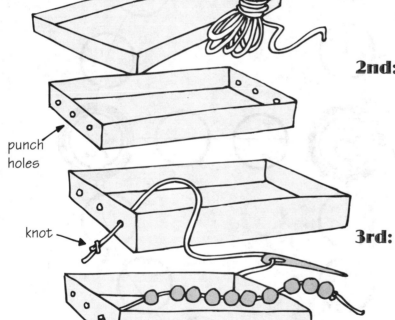

punch holes

knot

Here's a great opportunity to review place value! To use their abacus, have your students push all the beads to the left. As they count or add, move the beads to the right. Have them try counting a large pile of beads or adding simple math problems! If possible, try to locate someone who can demonstrate more complex operations with abacuses!

Putung Putung

People in Korea have traditionally enjoyed entertaining themselves at home through very simple means. On these quiet evenings, Putung Putung is often played by Korean children. *Putung* is actually a Chinese word that describes the sound a frog makes when it hits the water of a pond–similiar to the English word *plop*. So it would be fair to say that this game could be called Plop Plop.

To prepare for this game, arrange your class so that the students are sitting in chairs in a circle facing the center. The leader begins by saying, "One frog." The next player to their right says, "Two eyes." The third player says, "Four legs" and the fourth player says, "Putung!" The fifth player beckons the frog by saying, "Jump in the water." Here comes the tricky part. Your students now start the series with "Two frogs," hence, "Four eyes" and "Eight legs" and "Putung! Putung!" But, to complicate the game slightly, just one call of "Jump in the water." At the beginning of each round, another frog is added which multiplies all the other numbers in the series. If a player says the wrong number or the wrong order, they "putung" to the floor and are out of the game. If you'd like to keep all your students engaged in the game, penalize players who say the wrong number or order with a point. In this instance, the player with the least amount of points at the end of the game would be declared the winner. Happy putung-ing!

Speech bubbles: "One frog." "Two eyes." "Four legs." "Putung!"

Side tab: **Korean Culture**

75

Shuttlecock

Remember when Hackey Sacks were all the rage? If you don't, we're sure students will! Hackey Sack has been played in Korea for over 2,000 years, only Koreans call it Shuttlecock. In Korea, Shuttlecock is played using a weight or ball attached to feathers. Today's Hackey Sackers play for fun and agility, but Korean market merchants used to play Shuttlecock to keep their feet warm on cold days. The object of the game is to keep the shuttlecock in the air as long as possible using only your feet. This game has also been played in England with a slight twist . . . the shuttlecock is bounced between players using Ping-Pong™ paddles. The game is then called Battledore.

To play Shuttlecock, your students can bring in a Hackey Sack, or you can use a beanbag or small rubber ball. If you'd like your shuttlecock to be more authentic, use a Styrofoam™ or cork ball. First, drill or nail holes into the ball—one for each feather. Then glue a feather into each hole. To keep the ball from falling apart, wrap it with cloth tape or book binding tape. Finally, paint the ball a bright color. Your students now have a Korean Hackey Sack!

To start the game, one player throws the shuttlecock in the air. Before the shuttlecock hits the ground, one player must kick it back up into the air so that the game continues. Score is kept by counting the number of times the shuttlecock is hit without touching the ground. This game can be played solo or in a group. If Ping-Pong™ paddles are added, the same rules apply. After a few rounds of Shuttlecock, you may revive Hackey Sacking at your school!

In Korea, su-pok is a symbol expressing best wishes. This symbol consists of two Korean letters: *Su* meaning "long life" and *pok* meaning "happiness." The letters are often written in calligraphy, which traditionally is a form of writing done with a brush. The su-pok letters are found on clothing, furniture, screens and decorations. Provide your students with construction paper to make su-pok cards. Have them fold the paper in half. Place copies of the su-pok letters provided below so that they can refer to the symbols as they make their own cards. Once your students have copied the symbols on the outside of the card, encourage them to write a best wishes greeting on the inside. Then your students can exchange su-pok cards with other classmates, friends or family!

Bong! Bong! Bong! Let's Make a Korean Bell!

If you would like to see a bell that is 10 feet (3 m) high and over 1,000 years old, you should travel to Korea and view the Emille Bell. Many visitors go to see this bronze bell which is the largest example of its kind. Bell-making is one of the best-known metal crafts in Korea and a very pleasing one to the ear! These huge old bells make deep, rich sounds. The bells are traditionally decorated with lotus flowers, birds, plants and animals. Throughout Korea, you can still find these bells in temples. If your travel plans are for the last day of the year, then you will have the pleasure of hearing town mayors ring their local bell. If you or your students have any bells at home, you may want to bring the bells in to introduce your discussion about Korean bells and the sounds that they make.

Materials

Your students can create a smaller, quieter imitation of these bells in your classroom with an aluminum can (approximately 15 oz. [450 ml], the standard vegetable size), a large wooden bead, yarn, tagboard, crayons, scissors, hole punch and glue. Obviously the can should be clean, empty and already have the lid and label carefully removed. Try to avoid sharp edges.

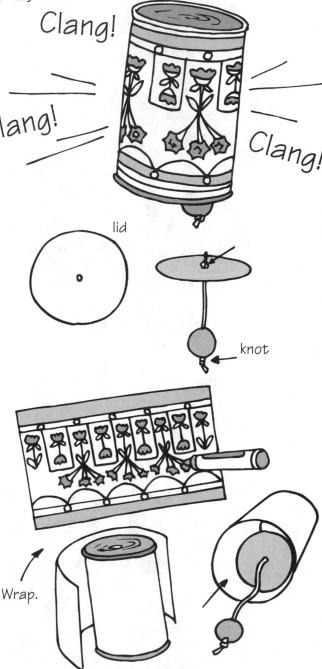

Clang!

Clang!

Clang!

lid

knot

Wrap.

Procedure

1st: Have your students trace and cut the lid pattern from the Let's Make a Korean Bell reproducible (page 79) onto tagboard. Punch a hole in the middle of the tagboard.

2nd: Pull one end of an approximately 4" (10 cm) piece of yarn through the tagboard and knot. Knot the other end to the wooden bead. This will create the clapper. Now have your students color the decorative label for the can/bell found on the reproducible. After they have cut out their new label, have them carefully glue the label to the can.

3rd: Finally, glue the tagboard cutout to the inside of the can's bottom so that the clapper hangs down. Push the tagboard to the bottom of the can with a pencil, and hold it there to dry. Although these bells won't "Bong! Bong! Bong!" you should hear "Clang! Clang! Clang!"

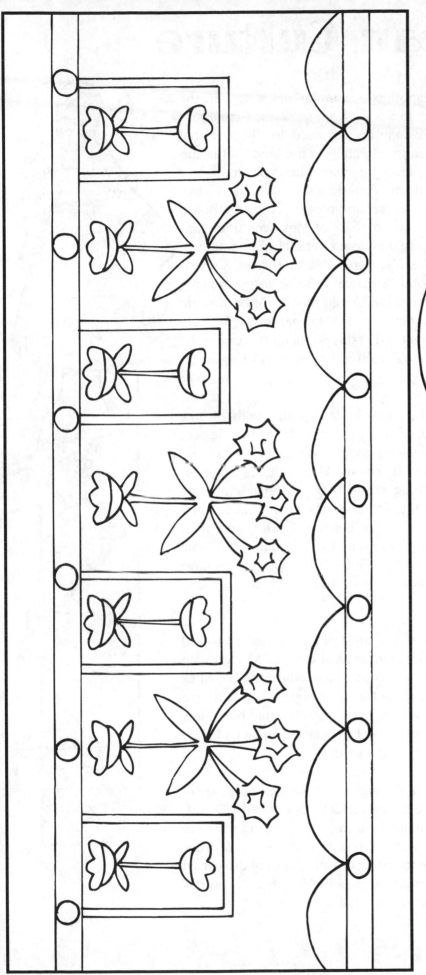

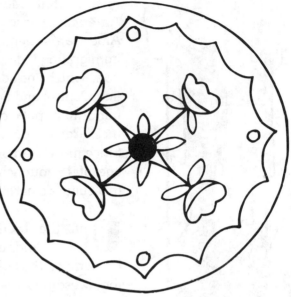

Korean Culture

Mexican Culture

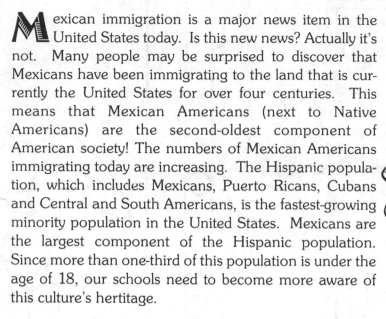

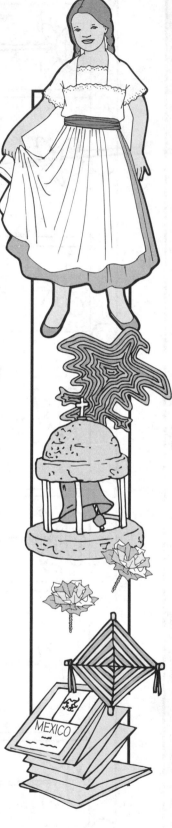

Mexican immigration is a major news item in the United States today. Is this new news? Actually it's not. Many people may be surprised to discover that Mexicans have been immigrating to the land that is currently the United States for over four centuries. This means that Mexican Americans (next to Native Americans) are the second-oldest component of American society! The numbers of Mexican Americans immigrating today are increasing. The Hispanic population, which includes Mexicans, Puerto Ricans, Cubans and Central and South Americans, is the fastest-growing minority population in the United States. Mexicans are the largest component of the Hispanic population. Since more than one-third of this population is under the age of 18, our schools need to become more aware of this culture's hertitage.

Until the 1500s, many Indian groups with diverse social and economic systems lived in Mexico. Remember those lessons about the mighty Mayas and the awesome Aztecs? Before the United States was even a glimmer of a thought, the Mexicans had elaborate urban centers with developed religious, political and commercial systems. The Hernán Cortez and then Spaniards arrived in Mexico in 1519, bringing their culture with them. Since the 1500s, these two groups have fused together to form a unique blend of Spanish and Indian traditions.

Today, Mexico is working towards an industrialized economy. The stereotypical view of Mexico as a slow-paced country with a subsistence farming base has little basis in reality since the economy is mainly driven by petroleum and tourism; not to mention that two-thirds of the people in Mexico now live in cities. In fact, Mexico City is the largest city in the world!

By teaching your students about the rich hertitage of the Mexican and the Mexican American cultures, your students will understand that this growing minority population has a wealth of history and tradition. Your students will be able to appreciate the depth of the varied cultures of the six main regions of Mexico and the cultures that have sprung from them.

Abuela by Arthur Dorros (Dutton Children's Books)

. . . And Now Miguel by Joseph Krumgold (T. Crowell)

The Cat in the Hat Beginner Dictionary in Spanish by Seuss (Random)

Cesar Chavez by R. Franchere (Harper & Row)

Class President by Johanna Hurwitz (Morrow)

Count Your Way Through Mexico by J. Haskins (Carolrhoda Books)

Diego by Jeanette Winter (Alfred A. Knopf)

The Dream Stair by Betsy James (Harper)

Everett Anderson's Friend by Lucille Clifton (Henry Holt)

A Family in Mexico by Tom Moran (Lerner Pub. Co.)

Famous Mexican Americans by Janet Morey (Cobblehill/Dutton)

Fiesta! Cinco de Mayo by June Behrens (Children's Book Press)

Flip-Flop Girl by Katherine Paterson (Dutton/Lodestar)

Gilberto and the Wind by Mary Hall Ets (Viking Press)

Hector Lives in the United States Now by Joan Hewett (Lippincott)

Hello, Amigos! by T. Brown (Henry Holt & Co.)

Hi by Ann Scott (Philomel)

Hill of Fire by Thomas Lewis (Harper & Row)

I Speak English for My Mom by M. Stanek (Albert Whitman & Co.)

Juan Patricio by B. Todd (G.P. Putnam's Sons)

Lito and the Clown by L. Politi (Charles Scribner's Sons)

Manuela's Birthday by L. Bannon (Albert Whitman & Co.)

The Mexicans in America by Jane Pinchot (Lerner)

My Best Friend Martha Rodriguez by Dianne MacMillan (Messner)

Nine Days to Christmas by Mary Hall Ets (Viking Press)

The One Who Came Back by Joann Mazzio (Houghton)

Rosa by L. Politi (Charles Scribner's Sons)

Rosa's Special Garden by Dale H. Fife (Albert Whitman & Co.)

Santiago by P. Belpre (Frederick Warne & Co.)

Secret City, U.S.A. by Felice Holman (Scribner)

The Silver Whistle by Ann Tompert (Macmillan Publishing Co.)

Something Special for Me by Vera B. Williams (Greenwillow Books)

Too Many Tamales by Gary Soto (Putnam)

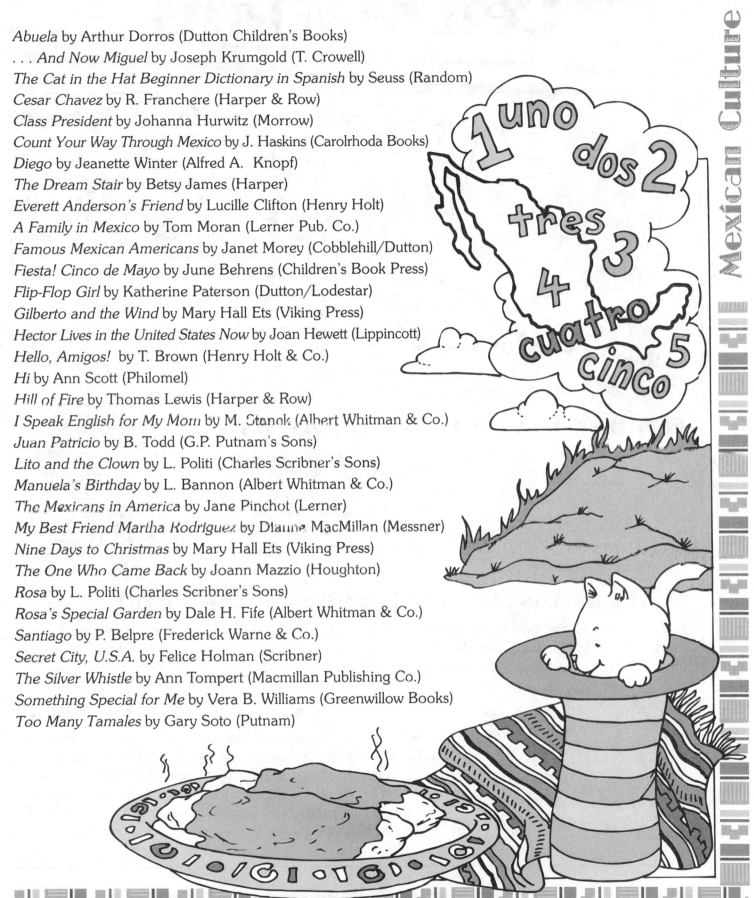

Celebrations

Cinco de Mayo

In Mexico on May 5, 1862, Mexican soldiers were victorious over the French in the Battle of Puebla. This holiday honors that victory. In Mexico and in the southwestern part of the United States, there are parades and reenactments of the famous battle with the French. People celebrate or have a fiesta. Mariachis play guitars, piccolos and violins; traditional folk dancers perform, and children enjoy breaking a piñata.

Day of the Race

On October 12, Spanish-speaking people the world over celebrate to remember their common heritage in both language and traditions.

El Grito (Mexican Independence Day)

Mexico won its independence from Spain in 1821, but on the morning of September 16, 1810, a priest named Miguel Hidalgo shouted out for Mexican independence while ringing the bell in his church. Mayors from every town in Mexico read the Declaration of Independence on the 15th and the following day the President of Mexico rings the same bell that Father Hidalgo rang in 1810. This day is celebrated with military parades, band concerts and fireworks.

El Día de Los Muertos (The Day of the Dead)

This holiday is also known as All Saints and Souls Day. It is similiar to traditions in Italy, Spain and parts of the United States. In Mexico, this holiday, which has Aztec and Mayan embellishments, occurs on November 1st and 2nd. On this day the dead are remembered with candy, baked goods, gifts and toys.

Las Posadas (The Inns)

During the Chistmas season from December 16 to 24, the story of Mary and Joseph's travels from inn to inn in order to find shelter is dramatized. Posadas, or groups of people searching for lodging, parade down the street to a fiesta that culminates with the breaking of a piñata. In the cities today, many Mexican children recieve gifts. Instead of Christmas trees, Mexican children have a Nacimiento or nativity scene.

Rima de Gallos (The Cock Fight)

In Mexico, sports involving animals are popular. Horse racing, bullfighting and cockfighting bring cries of "Vita! Vita" (pronounced Faster! Faster!) Here's a way your students can replicate cockfighting while reinforcing the Spanish words for colors.

For the cockfight, your students will need assorted colors of construction paper or felt and safety pins. Begin the game by asking your students to sit in a circle with a leader in the center. The leader chooses two players to be the cocks. The players stand facing away from each other while the leader pins on a different color of construction paper or felt on each of the player's backs. The leader yells, "Rima!" (pronounced Ree-ma) (Fight!), and the two players try to discover the color of the paper or felt on their opponent's back without allowing the other player to see theirs. No touching! The first player to call out the correct color wins! The winner then chooses a new leader, who in turn chooses new cocks. To make this game a little harder, teach your children the colors in Spanish, then require the winner to call out the correct color in Spanish.

black	= negro (nay-GROW)
blue	= azul (ah-ZOOL)
brown	= café (kah-FAY)
gray	= gris (grees)
green	= verde (bear-DAY)
orange	= naranja (nar-AN-ha)
pink	= rosado (row-SA-doe)
purple	= morado (more-AH-doe)
red	= rojo (row-HO)
white	= blanco (blan-CO)
yellow	= amarillo (am-ar-REE-yo)

Coyote and Sheep

Mexico has a long tradition of agarian life. This game which is ideal for 8-12 players, closely mimics the role of the shepherd protecting his flock. To begin, choose one shepherd and one coyote. The remaining players are the sheep. The sheep line up behind the shepherd (the shepherd is the first person in line) with their hands on the player's waist in front of them. When the coyote approaches the flock, the shepherd asks, "What do you want, Coyote?" The coyote replies, "I want a big, juicy sheep!" The shepherd then says, "The juiciest sheep are at the end of the line!" The coyote then tries to catch the last sheep. The shepherd's job is to keep the coyote away from the last lamb in his flock. The sheep must stay away from the coyote without letting go of the person in front of them. Once the coyote has caught the last sheep, the shepherd becomes the coyote, the first sheep becomes the shepherd and the coyote becomes the last sheep. (If you have a really slow coyote who is not able to catch the last sheep, try switching coyotes.)

Bolero Toy

Here's a great game for enhancing your students' hand-eye coordination. Bolero can mean a dance, a genre of music and a special kind of rope tie worn around the neck in this fun game. It is a word having several meanings or representatives.

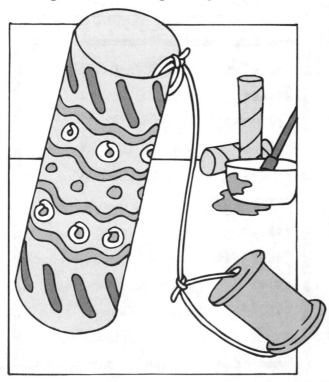

Before your class makes a Bolero toy, ask each student to bring in a toilet paper tube or a paper towel tube and an empty spool of thread into class. If students bring in the larger paper towel tubes, cut them in half. You will need to have a paper punch, paint, brushes and an 18" (46 cm) piece of yarn for each toy.

First, paint the tubes and let them dry. Your students can also paint the spools if they are wooden. Next, punch a hole in the tube close to the top. Then tie one end of the yarn to the spool and the other end to the tube. Your students are now ready to test their hand-eye coordination skills. The object of the Bolero game is to get the spool in the tube. Your students can have Bolero contests by counting the number of successes versus tries or by counting the number of successes in a specified time.

La Lotería (The Lottery)

If you travel through certain parts of Mexico on a Saturday or holiday, you might see adults playing a game that is similiar to bingo. The gameboards contain pictures of objects that have significance to Mexican culture. A "caller" chooses an object, then the players mark the pictures with corn or beans in attempt to cover all of the pictures. There's a twist to this game, however. When the caller chooses an object, he or she does not say the name, but rather gives a hint or says a poem about the object.

It is used for writing and it is made from wood.

This game works well in groups of six. After the groups have been formed, your students are ready to prepare the caller cards. Each student needs to create a poem or a hint for three pictures. Have each student record their hint on the small piece of paper and place it in the center of the table, facedown. For example, they may write *Ding! Dong!* for a bell or *You are bright; you shine in the night* for the moon.

Next, ask your students to cut out nine La Lotería gameboard pieces and tape them to their La Lotería gameboard. Each member of the group should have a different combination or configuration of pieces taped to their gameboard. There are many different gameboard pieces from which to choose.

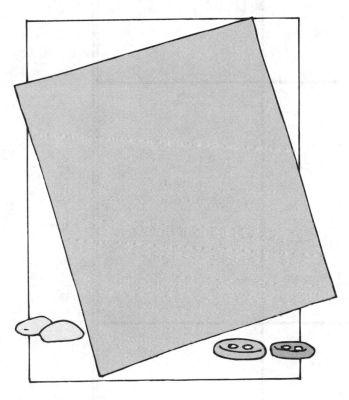

Before your class can begin playing La Lotería, they will need to make caller cards and gameboards. You will need to photocopy the La Lotería gameboard and La Lotería gameboard pieces (pages 86 and 87) for each student playing. In addition, your students will need a pencil, a small piece of paper, tape, scissors and popcorn kernels or beans.

Now your students are ready to play. A caller chooses one of the hints from the pile. Players match the clue with the picture using their corn or beans. The caller continues to read the hints or poems until a player has covered all of the pictures.

La Lotería

la computadora	**el escritorio**	**la ventana**	**la puerta**
la pluma	**el marcador**	**el color**	**el libro**
la bandera	**la sacapuntas**	**la calculadora**	**las tijeras**
la goma	**la regla**	**el borrador**	**la tiza**

God's Eye

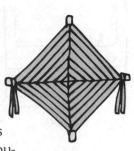

The Mexican culture has both Spanish and Indian roots. Most Mexicans today have both Spanish and Indian ancestry and speak Spanish, the national language. Yet there are still groups of Indians in Mexico who speak a dialect of the ancient Aztecs and practice their ancient religion. One of these groups of Indians are the Huichols who live in the Sierra Madres. They perform their traditional dances and make offerings to Father Sun, Grandfather Fire and other gods and goddesses. One of their offerings is the God's Eye which has become a popular good luck charm.

Materials

God's Eyes are made by weaving yarn over crossed sticks. Each student will need two craft sticks or 6" (15 cm) twigs, several colors of yarn and scissors.

Procedure

1st: Cross the two sticks at the centers and tie them together. The sticks should form a "+." Do not cut the yarn from the ball. To begin weaving, pull the yarn in front of any two sticks. Wrap the yarn around the front of the adjacent stick, loop the yarn under and around, then bring the yarn over the next adjacent stick. Continue wraping the sticks making sure that the yarn lies next to, not on top of, the yarn already wound.

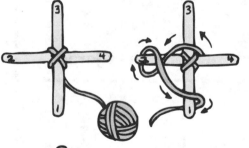

2nd: After several loops around each stick, your students will have created the "eye" and should change colors. Cut the yarn of the first color and tie it to the beginning of the second color behind the cross. Continue winding. Colors can be changed as often as your students want. Neatly tie the last thread to the end of one of the sticks.

3rd: Cut an additional 6" (15 cm) piece of yarn to make a loop for hanging. Finally, neatly tie the end of the 6" (15 cm) piece of yarn to the same stick. Your students may wish to make the loop for hanging long enough to wear the God's Eye as a beautiful good luck necklace.

Huíchol Yarn Pictures

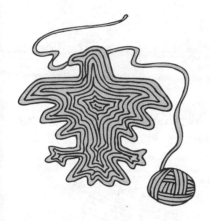

In addition to the God's Eye ornament, Huichol Indians also use yarn to make pretty pictures to retell their many myths and legends. When the Huichol make yarn pictures, a painter covers plywood with beeswax. After sitting several hours in the sun, the beeswax is soft enough to scratch a design into. The painter then presses strands of yarn into the beeswax, drawing a design that tells about their history and religion. Often Huichol legends contain brave heros or heroines or potent healing plants and animals. Many of these symbols appear in the yarn paintings.

Materials

Your students can make a Huichol yarn picture using a 6" x 6" (15 x 15 cm) piece of cardboard or tagboard, yarn, glue, scissors and pencils. Craft sticks are optional but make the activity easier. Warn your students that these paintings require patience as the glue needs time to dry. Using a minimal amount of glue and thick yarn will make this activity easier.

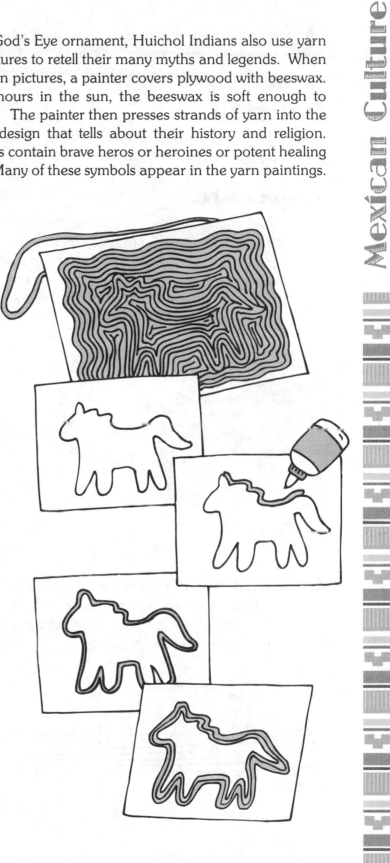

Procedure

1st: Have your students draw an outline of a animal, plant, person or shape in the middle of their cardboard.

2nd: Next, apply the glue along the outline that they have drawn. They may want to use a craft stick to press the yarn into place. Following the shape of the outline, spread another line of glue inside the shape. Again, apply the strands of yarn on top of the glue. Continue to outline each shape several times with glue and yarn. When your students have completed their designs, glue a border along the edges of the cardboard.

3rd: Finish the picture by filling yarn into the open spaces between the shapes in the middle and the outide border. Your students can glue a piece of yarn to the back of the cardboard to hang their picture on a bulletin board or wall!

Paper Flowers

A traditional craft of Mexico is the making of paper flowers out of colorful tissue paper. The flowers are made in various sizes, used in many ceremonies and even sold as gifts on street corners.

Materials

Assorted colors of tissue paper, rulers, hole punch, pipe cleaners, pencils and scissors

Procedure

1st: Use rulers to measure and cut the tissue paper into 5" x 5" (13 x 13 cm) squares. After they have measured and cut out the squares, they can trim them to make various sizes to eventually create the layered look of the flower petals.

2nd: Layer the various sized pieces of tissue paper on top of one another proceeding from the larger pieces on the bottom to the smaller pieces on the top.

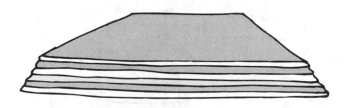

3rd: Use your hole punch to make two holes in the center of each stack of tissue paper.

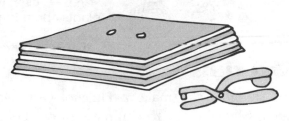

4th: Hand out the pipe cleaners to your students. Have students slide the pipe cleaner up one hole and then bend it around to fit down the other hole. Make sure the pipe cleaner is even on both sides and then twist the two ends together to make the stem.

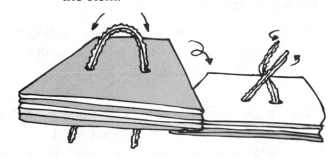

5th: Finally, have your students carefully arrange the tissue paper pieces to look like the petals of a well-shaped flower.

A Clever Codex

eed a new way to inspire your students to write? Try this activity! Making a codex is a clever way for your students to create their own book. The Aztecs of Mexico used a codex, or fold-out picture book, to keep records of their history, calendars and daily life. Although the Aztec scribes, or writers, kept their records using pictures and symbols, you can adapt this activity to your class.

Your students will need two pieces of blank white paper (8¹/₂" x 11" [22 x 28 cm]), two pieces of poster board (5" x 6" [13 x 15 cm]), pencils, markers, glue, tape and scissors. To begin, fold each piece of white paper in half lengthwise. Then cut along the creases to create four long sheets. Now, tape the long sheets together (front and back) on the short edges as shown. Next, fold the four long sheets back and forth widthwise so that the book will unfold like an accordion. Finally, to create book covers, glue the poster board pieces to the two end sheets of paper. Your students are now ready to decorate and write in their codex book!

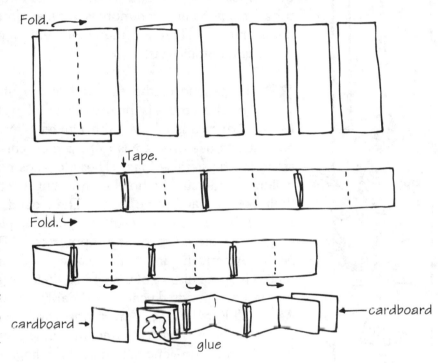

Have your students select a topic for their codex. Some students may want to draw guidelines with a ruler for their stories. Maybe your students would like to research Mexico or the Aztec, or perhaps write a report on the cultures that they have been studying, or write an imaginative story to correspond to a classroom unit. Codexes are flexible! They can include illustrations to make a clever and stunning presentation.

Native American Culture

Both information and stereotypes are easily available when discussing Native American cultures. Educators must be sensitive about presenting culturally valid and accurate resources for our children's learning. The activities that we have provided attempt to show that while Native Americans share some cultural similarities, each tribe has distinctly different beliefs and traditions. Native Americans are not a monolithic group. Each sub-group has its own way of cooking and dressing, has its own types of shelter and its own social structure. The tribes' religions and ceremonies vary, as do their beliefs about nature. There are many different languages with many different dialects!

Perhaps one of the similar features of the Native American tribes is the use of mythology and legend. Native Americans all over the United States used and continue to use these tools to help their children under-stand the mysteries of life. These legends not only help children understand who they are, but where they and their people have come from. The legends record the dreams, hopes, fears and suffering of a people who have long been stereotyped and oppressed. By studying Native Americans and their cultures, your students will realize that the history of the United States is greater than the past two hundred years of primarily white civilization. As we all know, Native Americans were the first immi-grants to North America and this may have occurred 50,000 years ago–long before the founding of the United States.

Today Native Americans live all over the United States. They live in cities, towns, suburbs, in the countryside and on reservations. Some Native Americans still practice the traditional ways of living, while others have adopted modern ways of life. The Native American people paved the trails that our roads and railroads now follow, they cultivated the first food grown in this country, they gave us the names of many of our states, towns, rivers and lakes and have contributed to the growth of this country in innumerable ways. Perhaps the greatest gift you can give to your students when pre-senting this unit is a broadening of their understanding about Native Americans.

Annie and the Old One by Miska Miles (Joy Street/Little/Brown)

Arrow to the Sun by Gerald McDermott (Viking)

Baby Rattlesnake by Te Ata (Children's Press)

Beyond the Ridge by Paul Goble (Bradbury)

Black Elk by Carol Greene (Children's Press)

Bring Back the Deer by Jeffrey Prusski (Gulliver/Harcourt)

Buffalo Dance by Nancy Van Laan (Joy Street/Little/Brown)

Caddie Woodlawn by Carol Brink (Macmillan)

The Courage of Sarah Noble by Alice Dalgliesh (Aladdin/Macmillan)

The Discovery of the Americas by Betsy Maestro (Lothrop)

Dreamplace by George Lyon (Orchard)

Dream Wolf by Paul Goble (Bradbury)

Fire Race by Jonathan London (Chronicle)

The Ghost and the Lone Warrior by Carrie Taylor
    (Children's Press)

The Gift of the Sacred Dog by Paul Goble (Bradbury)

Goat in the Rug by Charles L. Blood and Martin Link
    (Four Winds)

Her Seven Brothers by Paul Goble (Bradbury)

How Raven Brought Light to People by Ann Dixon
    (McElderry)

How We Came to the Fifth World by H. Rohmer
    (Children's Press)

Iktomi and the Berries by Paul Goble (Orchard)

Island of the Blue Dolphins by Scott O'Dell
    (Houghton)

Julie of the Wolves by Jean George (HarperTrophy)

The Legend of El Dorado by Beatriz Vidal (Knopf)

Ma'll and Cousin Horned Toad by S. Begay (Scholastic/Hardcover)

Meet Tricky Coyote! by Gretchen Mayo (Walker)

Monster Slayer by Vee Browne (Northland)

Mystery of Navajo Moon by Timothy Green
    (Northland)

Nessa's Fish by Nancy Luenn (Atheneum)

Pocahontas by Carol Greene (Children's Press)

Raven by Gerald McDermott (Harcourt)

The Rough-Face Girl by Rafe Martin (Putnam)

The Sign of the Beaver by Elizabeth George Speare (Dell)

That Tricky Coyote! by Gretchen Mayo (Walker)

The Trees Stand Shining by Hettie Jones (Dial)

The Winter Solstice by Ellen Jackson (Millbrook Press)

Native American Culture

Celebrations

Harvest Festival

Provide an opportunity to acknowledge the Native American respect and reverence for nature and the land during the fall season. This festival can be separate from traditional Halloween or Thanksgiving.

Indian Day of Glory

On June 25 we commemorate the Battle of the Little Big Horn. In 1876 the Cheyenne and Sioux Indian tribes defeated Colonel George Custer and the 7th cavalry.

New Year

Native Americans used the seasons to determine their calendar. The Choctaw celebrate the New Year during late July or early August when the corn ripens. The Green Corn Dance is performed to insure a year of peace. During this time, old fires were extinguished and new fires were lit. Past grudges among people in the tribe were forgotten so that the year could start with a new beginning.

Gallup Inter-Tribal Indian Ceremonial

During mid-August in Gallup, New Mexico, the Inter-Tribal Ceremonial is hosted. Dressed in authentic costumes, about 500 Indian dancers demonstrate their tribes' dancing customs. This celebration also contains a fair with races, handicrafts, parades and sports. There are many tribal celebrations throughout the U.S. Perhaps you and your students can find out about one in your area.

Shalako Festival

On December 1, the Zuni Indians in New Mexico honor the Shalako, the messengers of the rain spirits. These Indians cherish every drop of rain since they grow corn on their desert land. The Zuni men dance, chant and pray wearing masks to represent the rain spirits and bells tied to their ankles and knees.

Hopi Snake Dance

In late August the Hopi Snake Dance ceremony is held. This is the most famous ceremony of the Hopi Indian tribe.

National American Indian Heritage Month

In 1990 the President of the United States declared November as the official month in which to celebrate Native Americans.

Inuit Indian Ball Pass

The Inuits of the Artic Region of North America have a special ball-passing game that your children will enjoy. The Inuits used to make a 3" to 4" (8 to 10 cm) diameter ball out of sealskin hide by filling it with sand. For your purposes, any soft small-sized ball will do. Have your students kneel in a circle. Explain to them that they are going to pass the ball around the circle as fast as they possibly can. Also tell them that when they touch the ball they must not grasp it with their fingers. As a matter of fact, the Inuits play this game by making sure that they have a flat, open-palm hand when passing the ball. So special balancing skills will be needed, as well as quick reflexes. Once your students become really good at passing one ball around the circle with flat, open palms, introduce another ball so that two balls can be passed around at the same time.

Native American Ball Race

Ready for some fast-paced action in your classroom? Challenge your students to this variation of a favorite footsie game of the Native Americans. First, arrange your classroom so that the desks make rows that are wide enough for two students to walk between (pushing a ball, that is). Next, divide your class into tribes of six players each. Three players should stand at one end of the row of desks and the remaining three at the other. You will need one ball for each tribe. At your signal, the players must push, not kick, the balls between the rows of desks without letting the ball stray. Any ball that wanders underneath a desk must be brought back to the starting line. When a player reaches the end of a row, he or she sits down and the next player pushes the ball back to the start. The tribe that has all of its members push the ball up the path first wins. Remember, absolutely no kicking!

The Stick Game

Are there any good guessers in your class? Yes? Great! Your students will love this game. First, you will need to collect 12 pencils to use as sticks. To begin the game, have one student hold the pencils behind their back. He decides how to distribute the pencils between his two hands. Each of the other students takes a guess as to how many pencils are hidden in each hand. If six students try and fail, the pencil holder wins the game. If a student is clever enough to guess correctly, she becomes the pencil holder and the game begins again.

Here's another Native American stick game adapted for your room. You will only need one pencil for this version of the game, but you will also need four piles of construction paper that have been shredded–enough to cover a pencil. First, divide your students into two tribes. Have your students sit in a circle around the piles of paper. The game begins by passing the pencil from player to player around the circle. Any player at anytime may step into the middle of the circle and try to hide the pencil in one of the piles. Since all the other players will be watching them like a hawk, they must be a very sneaky and try to conceal the pencil with quick hand movements. The student's objective is to trick the other team. The leader of the team tries to guess the correct pile. If they are right, one point is scored. If the leader is wrong, the tribe hiding the pencil receives the point. The first team with five points wins!

Plains Indian Vest

An important part of exploring a people is to identify and create the traditional clothing of that culture. The Plains Indians would wear clothing made from buffalo hide or deerskin to protect their skin from the intense sun. It might be difficult to get an animal hide, but it's easy to get the next best thing . . . paper bags!

Materials

One brown paper grocery bag for each student, scissors, yarn, hole punch and various colors of tempera

Procedure

1st: Hand out one large plain brown paper grocery bag to each student. You can get them, of course, at your local grocery store (they're usually more than willing to give the bags out to teachers), or ask students to bring bags from home.

2nd: Have your students take their scissors and cut up the center of the front of the bag until they come to the bottom. Then have your students cut a hole on the bottom of the bag for the neckline. Then have your students cut circles on the sides of the bag for their arms.

3rd: Have your students cut along the opening of the bag to make the fringe typically found on Native Americans' vests.

4th: Invite your students to punch one hole on both sides of the center cut near the neckline. These holes will be for the ties. After the holes have been cut, pass a thick piece of yarn through each hole, and tie a knot at both ends. The knot will keep the yarn from falling through the holes.

5th: Now students can adorn their paper bag vests using the tempera paint. Show your students various Native American designs, and invite them to paint those designs on their vests.

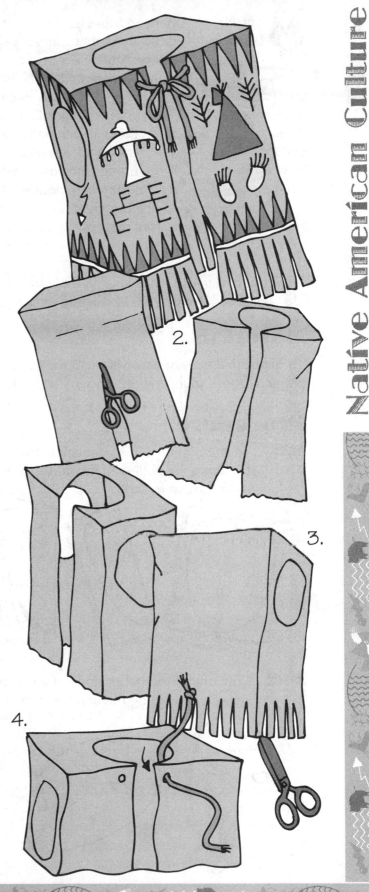

2.

3.

4.

Native American Masks

Many Native American tribes have a rich tradition of making masks. Animal masks were often worn because it was believed that animal spirits would help to make the wearers strong and brave. Native Americans in Alaska admired the strength of the brown bear, hence many bear masks have been discovered and preserved. Other Native Americans believed in spirits that resided in natural forces. The Iroquois would make masks to encourage the spirit-that-helps-people-who-travel-through-forests to protect them. The Native Americans who lived in the dry southwest would make masks to summon the rain spirit to come water their crops. Today, many masks and costumes are used to help these people remember their traditions during ceremonies. Your children will love to learn the history behind masks before creating their own. To begin your lesson, discuss why Native Americans used masks.

This activity also lends itself to recognizing symmetry and assymmetry. Be sure to discuss this with your students when constructing their masks.

Materials

To begin this activity you will need the Native American Mask reproducible (page 100), construction paper, scissors, glue, crayons and a 1" x 11" (2.5 x 28 cm) strip of construction paper for each mask.

Procedure

1st: To start, have your students fold the reproducible in half widthwise. With the paper still folded, cut along the outline of the mask. Next, ask your students to mark and cut out an eye (the paper must remain folded!).

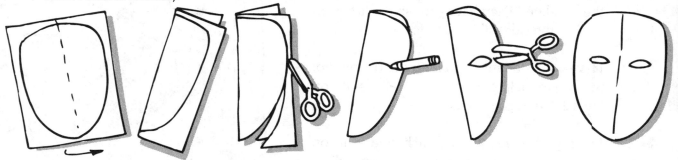

2nd: Now unfold the paper and cut along the center crease from the bottom to the nose. By over-lapping and gluing the bottom of the mask, you will create a face-fitting mask.

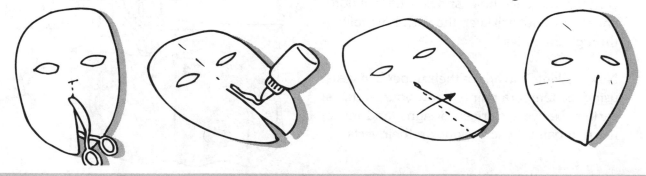

3rd: Your students are now ready to get creative! They can use additional pieces of construction paper to add noses that protrude, a mouth, eyelashes, hair, face paint or whatever their imaginations can generate!

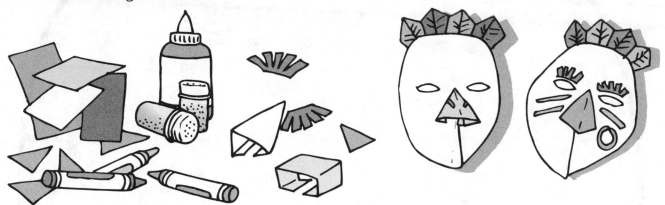

4th: When your students have finished embellishing their masks, glue the 1" x 11" (2.5 x 28 cm) strip of construction paper to each side of the mask. After the glue dries, they are ready to proudly wear their creations.

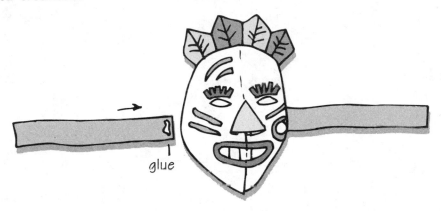

glue

5th: For the more advanced mask makers, invite your students to draw freehand their own mask outline on a piece of paper that is folded in half.

Native American Culture

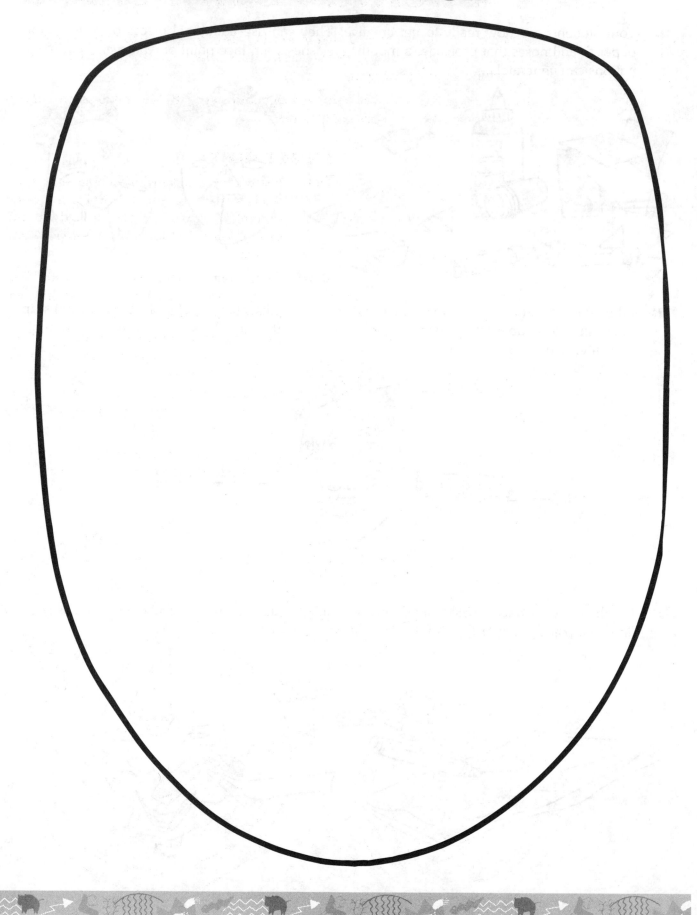

Native American Spirit Shield

Native Americans who lived on the Plains not only used masks, but also used shields to summon special spirits. Before going off to battle, Plains Indians would make leather shields to protect themselves. They would adorn the shield with pictures of protective spirits.

A shield pattern is provided on page 102. You will also need tagboard, yarn (18" [46 cm] for each student), markers, scissors, tape and a hole punch. Beads are optional.

Procedure

1st: Instruct your students to decorate their spirit shield with Native American designs. Several examples have been drawn around the out-side of the shield to help your students get started.

2nd: Once your students are happy with their design, have them cut out the circle and glue it onto a piece of circular tagboard.

3rd: Next, punch holes where indicated. Then wrap a piece of tape around the end of the yarn. Weave the yarn through the shield. If you have beads, string several beads on the yarn each time it appears on the outside face of the shield.

4th: Finally, tie the two ends of the yarn together. Your students are now ready for battle!

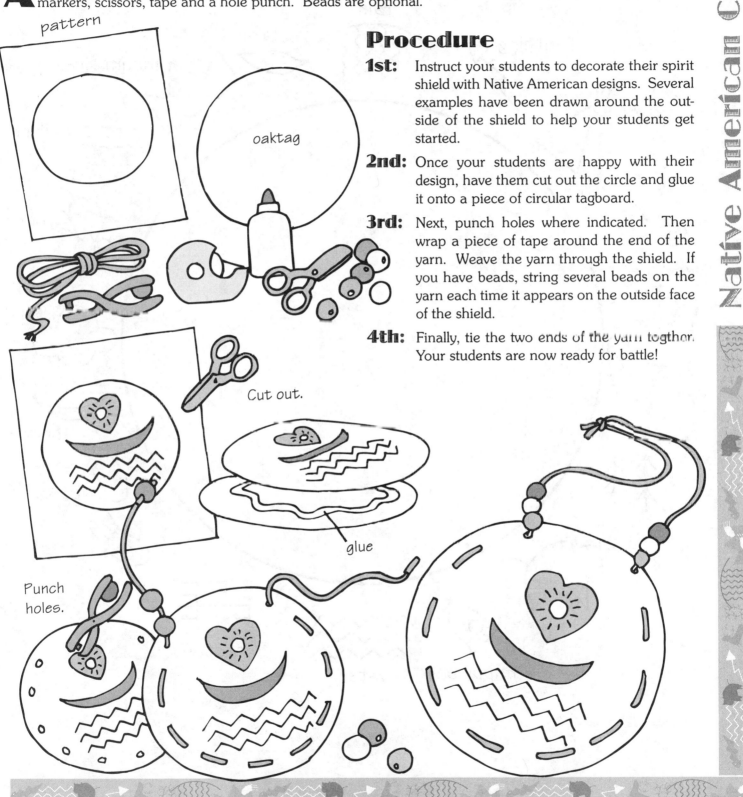

pattern

oaktag

Cut out.

glue

Punch holes.

Native American Spirit Shield

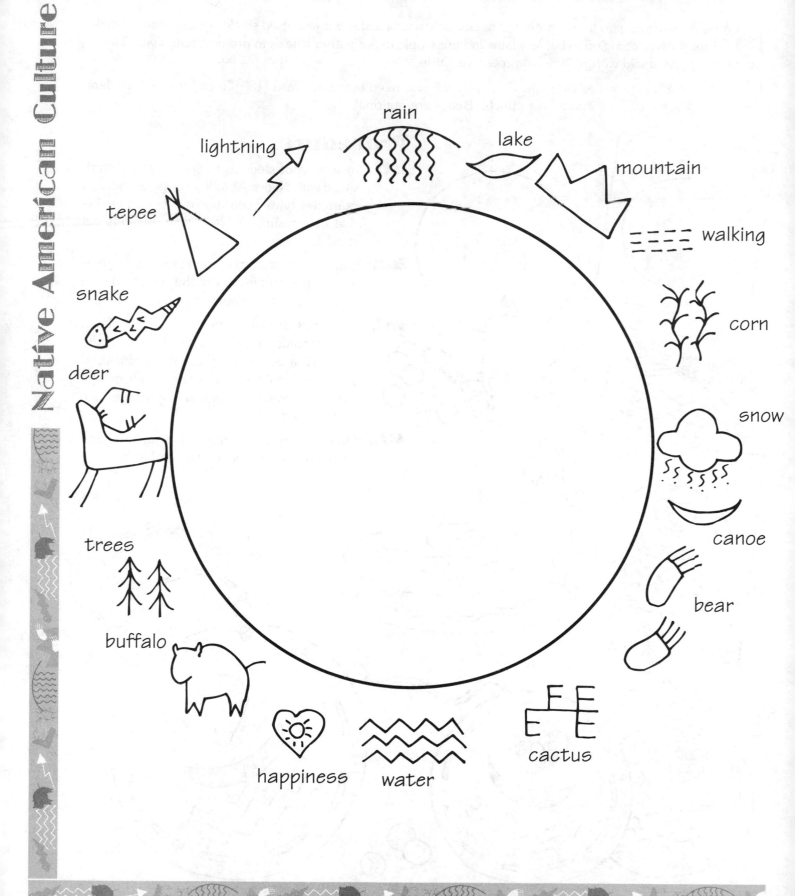

rain

lightning

lake

mountain

tepee

walking

snake

corn

deer

snow

canoe

trees

bear

buffalo

happiness

water

cactus

A Multicultural Museum

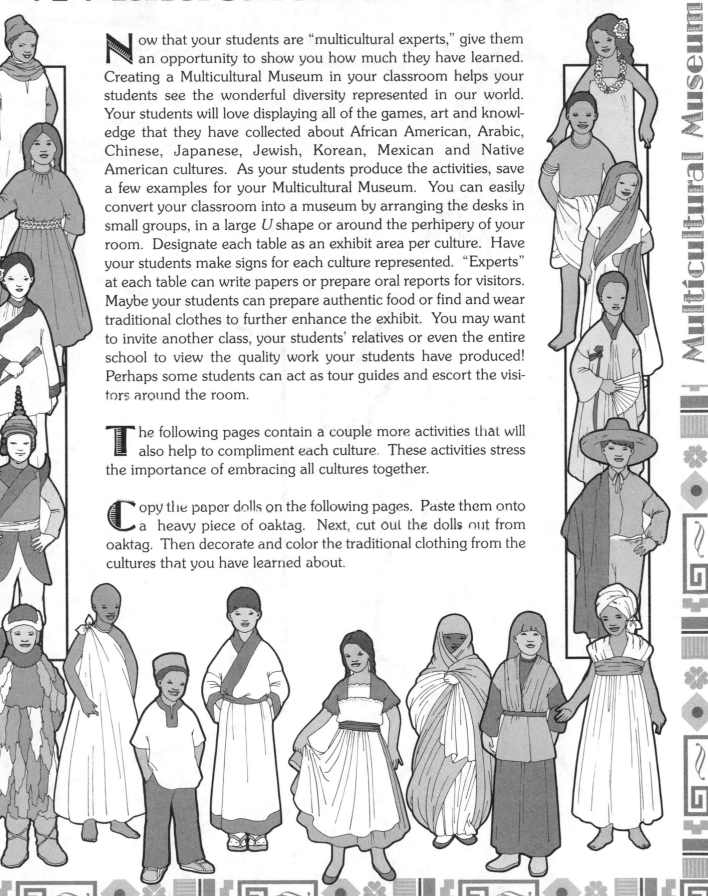

Now that your students are "multicultural experts," give them an opportunity to show you how much they have learned. Creating a Multicultural Museum in your classroom helps your students see the wonderful diversity represented in our world. Your students will love displaying all of the games, art and knowledge that they have collected about African American, Arabic, Chinese, Japanese, Jewish, Korean, Mexican and Native American cultures. As your students produce the activities, save a few examples for your Multicultural Museum. You can easily convert your classroom into a museum by arranging the desks in small groups, in a large *U* shape or around the perhipery of your room. Designate each table as an exhibit area per culture. Have your students make signs for each culture represented. "Experts" at each table can write papers or prepare oral reports for visitors. Maybe your students can prepare authentic food or find and wear traditional clothes to further enhance the exhibit. You may want to invite another class, your students' relatives or even the entire school to view the quality work your students have produced! Perhaps some students can act as tour guides and escort the visitors around the room.

The following pages contain a couple more activities that will also help to compliment each culture. These activities stress the importance of embracing all cultures together.

Copy the paper dolls on the following pages. Paste them onto a heavy piece of oaktag. Next, cut out the dolls out from oaktag. Then decorate and color the traditional clothing from the cultures that you have learned about.

Figure and Stand

1. Paste figure and stand onto oaktag.
2. Cut out.
3. Fold stand pattern along dotted lines.
4. Apply glue to stand where indicated.
5. Align stand with bottom of figure and attach.

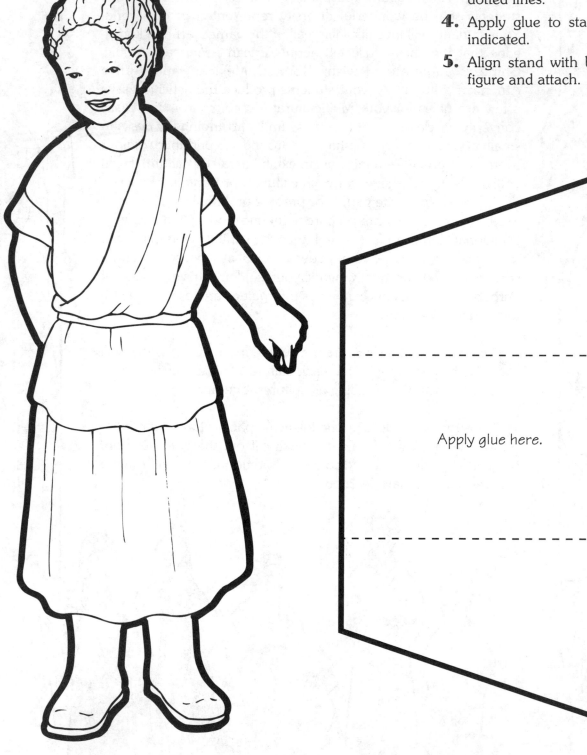

Apply glue here.

Figure and Stand

1. Paste figure and stand onto oaktag.

2. Cut out.

3. Fold stand pattern along dotted lines.

4. Apply glue to stand where indicated.

5. Align stand with bottom of figure and attach.

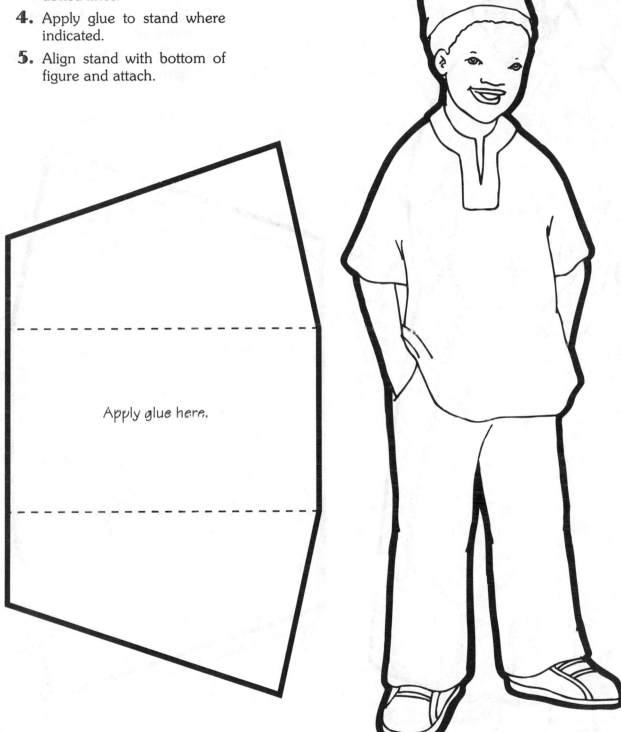

Apply glue here.

TLC10012 Copyright © Teaching & Learning Company, Carthage, IL 62321

Figure and Stand

1. Paste figure and stand onto oaktag.
2. Cut out.
3. Fold stand pattern along dotted lines.
4. Apply glue to stand where indicated.
5. Align stand with bottom of figure and attach.

Apply glue here.

Kenya Boy

106

Figure and Stand

1. Paste figure and stand onto oaktag.

2. Cut out.

3. Fold stand pattern along dotted lines.

4. Apply glue to stand where indicated.

5. Align stand with bottom of figure and attach.

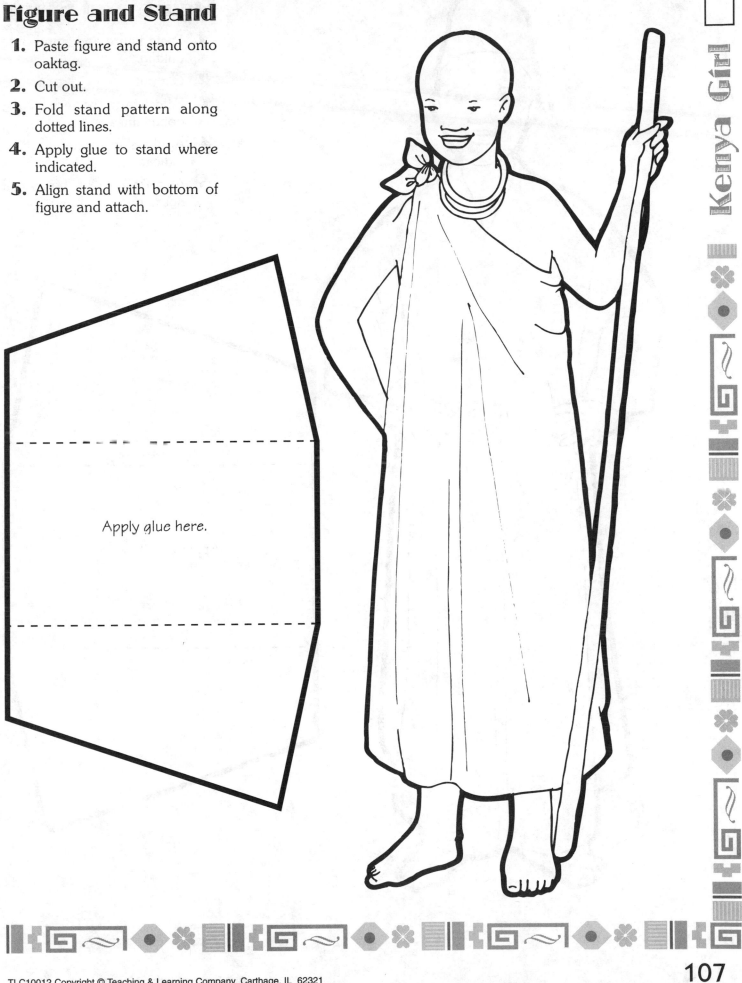

Apply glue here.

107

Figure and Stand

1. Paste figure and stand onto oaktag.
2. Cut out.
3. Fold stand pattern along dotted lines.
4. Apply glue to stand where indicated.
5. Align stand with bottom of figure and attach.

Apply glue here.

Figure and Stand

1. Paste figure and stand onto oaktag.

2. Cut out.

3. Fold stand pattern along dotted lines.

4. Apply glue to stand where indicated.

5. Align stand with bottom of figure and attach.

Apply glue here.

Figure and Stand

1. Paste figure and stand onto oaktag.
2. Cut out.
3. Fold stand pattern along dotted lines.
4. Apply glue to stand where indicated.
5. Align stand with bottom of figure and attach.

Apply glue here.

Figure and Stand

1. Paste figure and stand onto oaktag.

2. Cut out.

3. Fold stand pattern along dotted lines.

4. Apply glue to stand where indicated.

5. Align stand with bottom of figure and attach.

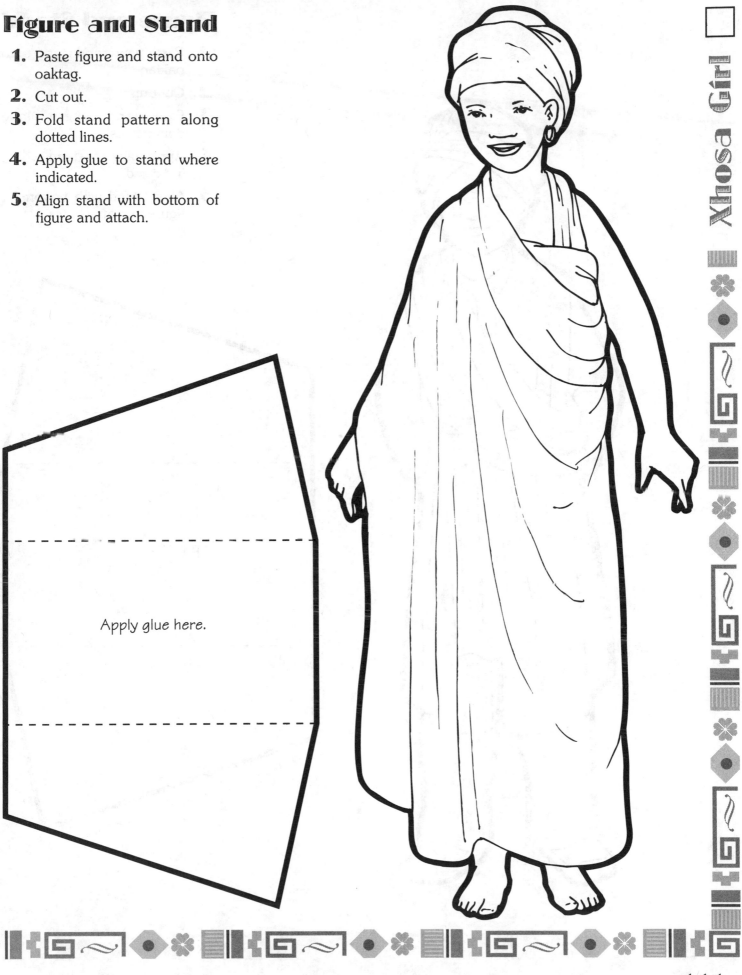

Apply glue here.

Figure and Stand

1. Paste figure and stand onto oaktag.

2. Cut out.

3. Fold stand pattern along dotted lines.

4. Apply glue to stand where indicated.

5. Align stand with bottom of figure and attach.

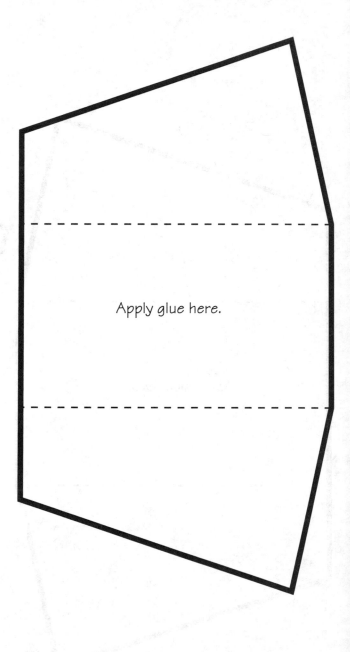

Apply glue here.

Figure and Stand

1. Paste figure and stand onto oaktag.
2. Cut out.
3. Fold stand pattern along dotted lines.
4. Apply glue to stand where indicated.
5. Align stand with bottom of figure and attach.

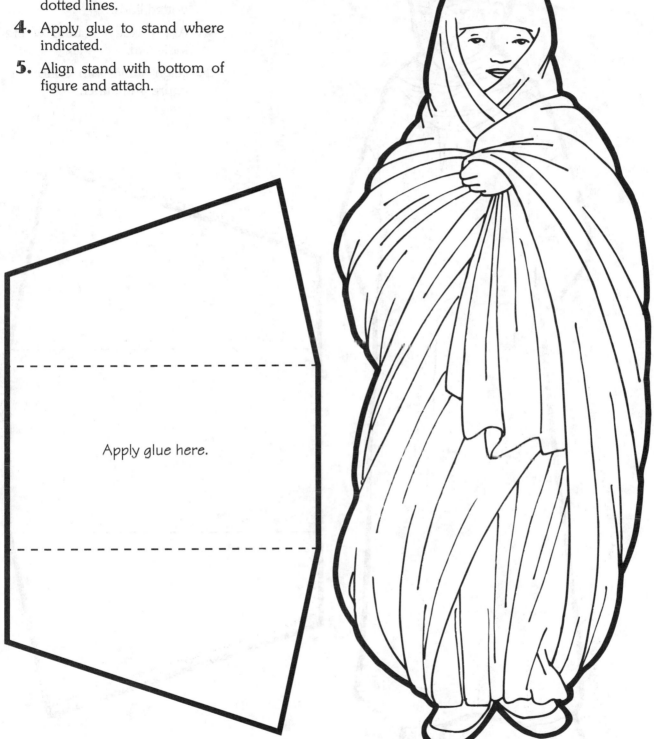

Apply glue here.

Figure and Stand

1. Paste figure and stand onto oaktag.

2. Cut out.

3. Fold stand pattern along dotted lines.

4. Apply glue to stand where indicated.

5. Align stand with bottom of figure and attach.

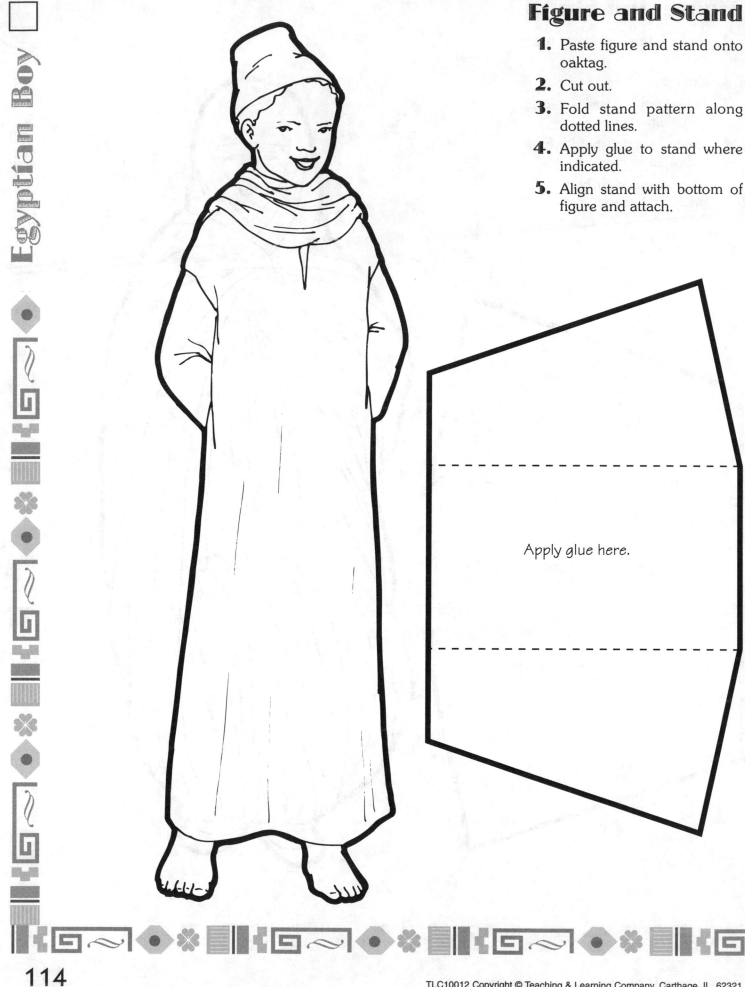

Apply glue here.

Figure and Stand

1. Paste figure and stand onto oaktag.
2. Cut out.
3. Fold stand pattern along dotted lines.
4. Apply glue to stand where indicated.
5. Align stand with bottom of figure and attach.

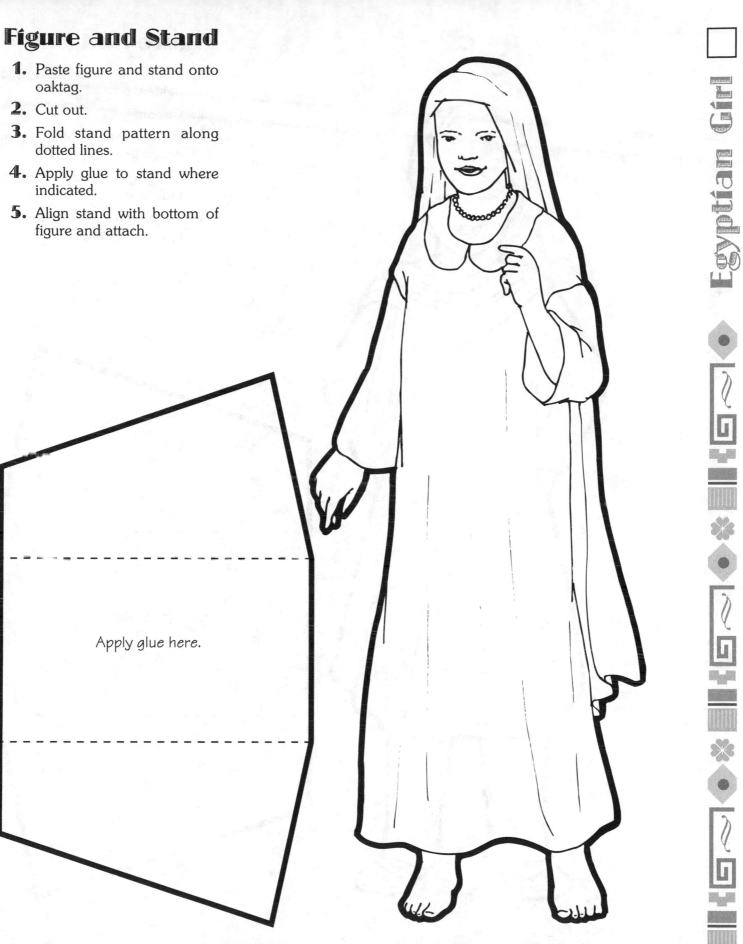

Apply glue here.

Figure and Stand

1. Paste figure and stand onto oaktag.

2. Cut out.

3. Fold stand pattern along dotted lines.

4. Apply glue to stand where indicated.

5. Align stand with bottom of figure and attach.

Apply glue here.

Figure and Stand

1. Paste figure and stand onto oaktag.

2. Cut out.

3. Fold stand pattern along dotted lines.

4. Apply glue to stand where indicated.

5. Align stand with bottom of figure and attach.

Apply glue here.

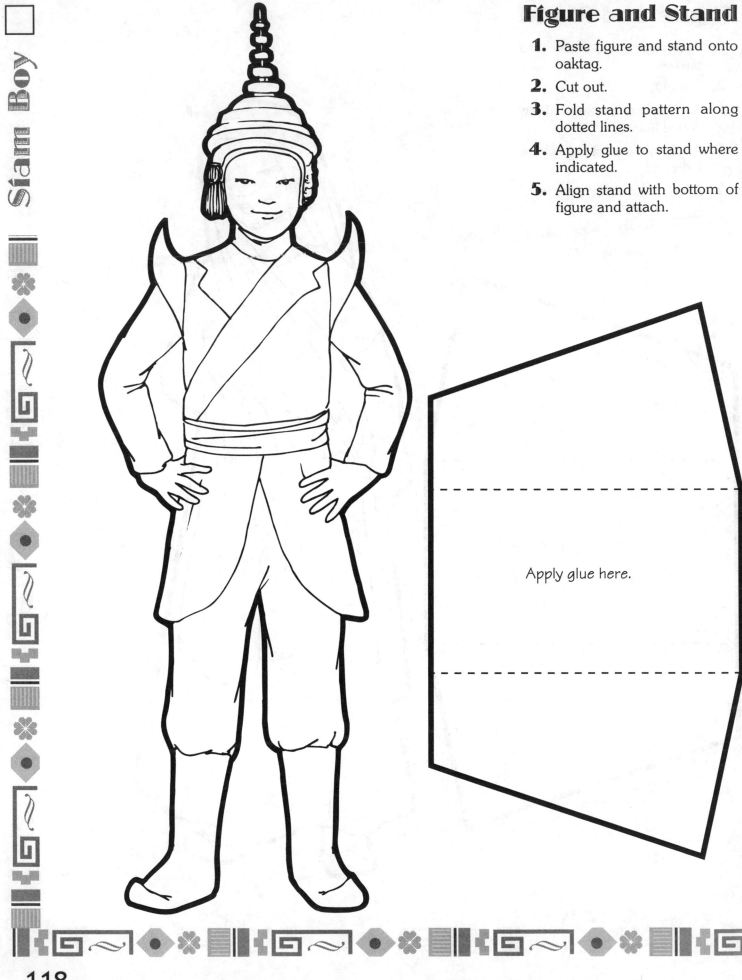

Figure and Stand

1. Paste figure and stand onto oaktag.
2. Cut out.
3. Fold stand pattern along dotted lines.
4. Apply glue to stand where indicated.
5. Align stand with bottom of figure and attach.

Apply glue here.

Figure and Stand

1. Paste figure and stand onto oaktag.
2. Cut out.
3. Fold stand pattern along dotted lines.
4. Apply glue to stand where indicated.
5. Align stand with bottom of figure and attach.

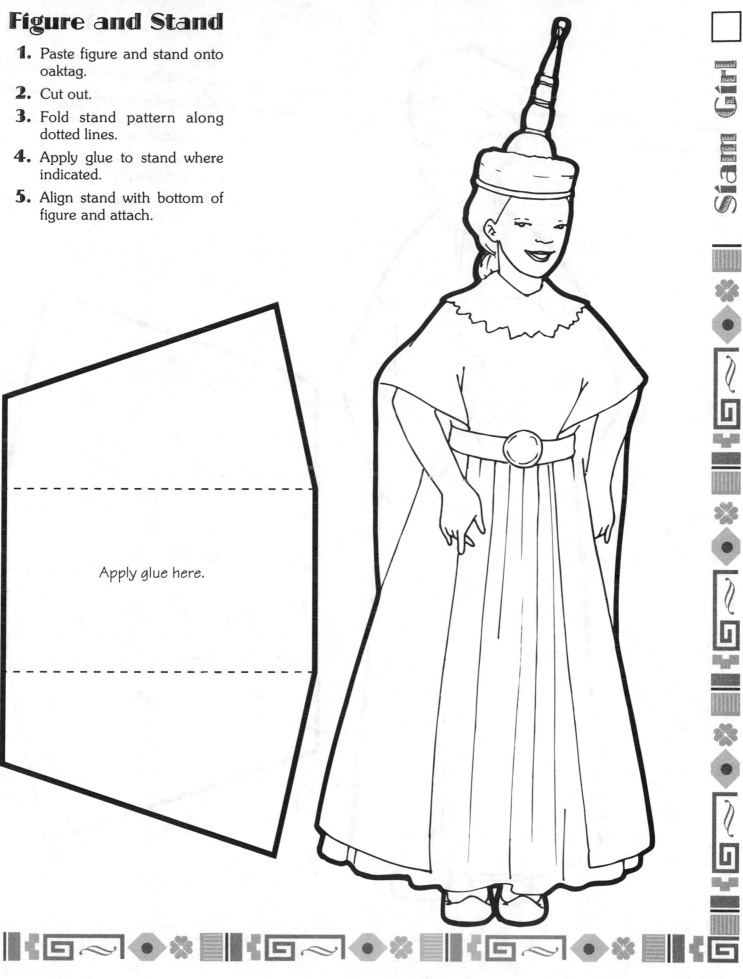

Apply glue here.

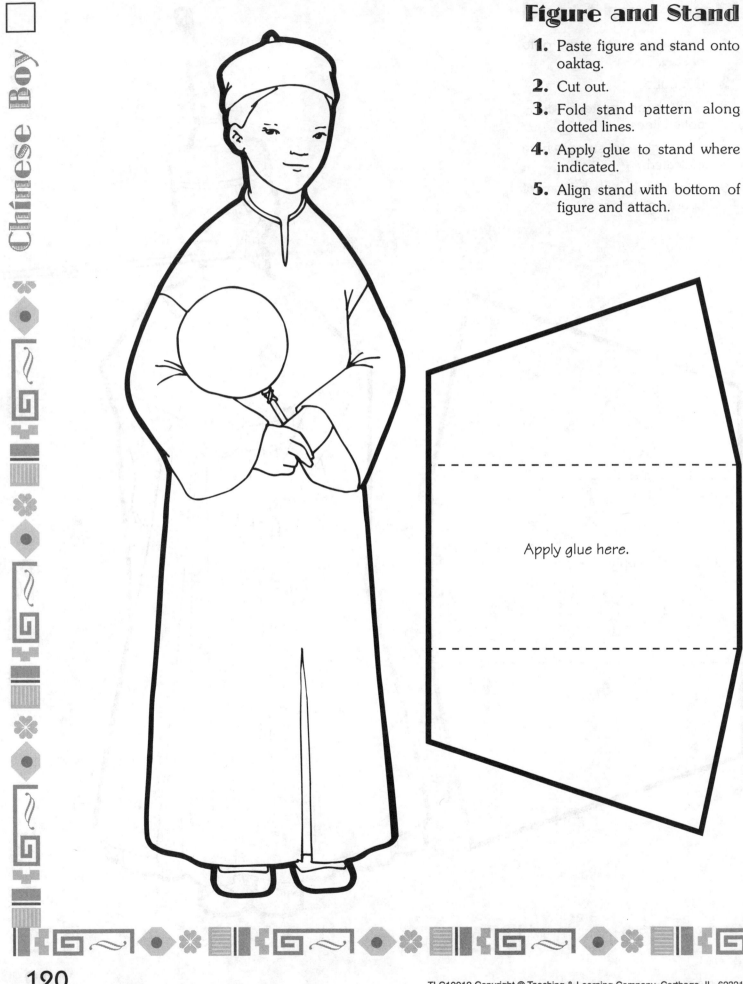

Figure and Stand

1. Paste figure and stand onto oaktag.
2. Cut out.
3. Fold stand pattern along dotted lines.
4. Apply glue to stand where indicated.
5. Align stand with bottom of figure and attach.

Apply glue here.

Figure and Stand

1. Paste figure and stand onto oaktag.
2. Cut out.
3. Fold stand pattern along dotted lines.
4. Apply glue to stand where indicated.
5. Align stand with bottom of figure and attach.

Apply glue here.

Figure and Stand

1. Paste figure and stand onto oaktag.

2. Cut out.

3. Fold stand pattern along dotted lines.

4. Apply glue to stand where indicated.

5. Align stand with bottom of figure and attach.

Apply glue here.

Figure and Stand

1. Paste figure and stand onto oaktag.
2. Cut out.
3. Fold stand pattern along dotted lines.
4. Apply glue to stand where indicated.
5. Align stand with bottom of figure and attach.

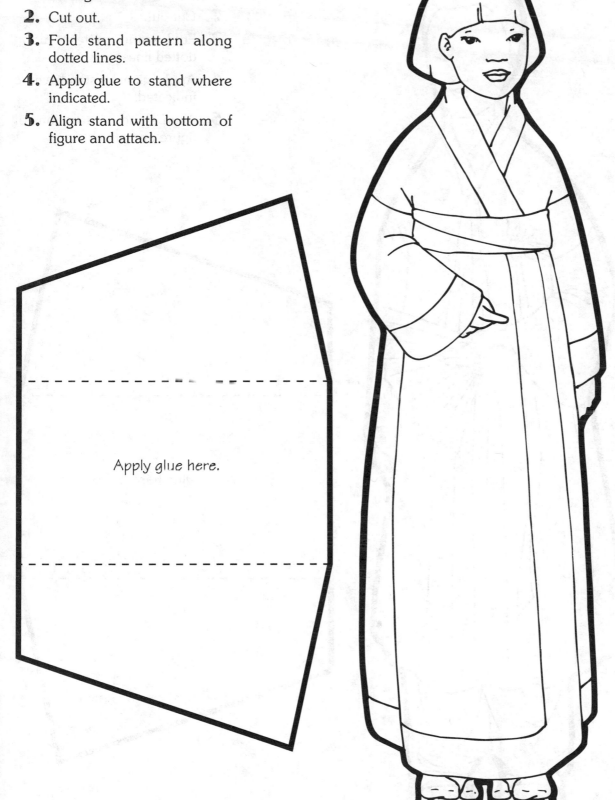

Apply glue here.

Figure and Stand

1. Paste figure and stand onto oaktag.
2. Cut out.
3. Fold stand pattern along dotted lines.
4. Apply glue to stand where indicated.
5. Align stand with bottom of figure and attach.

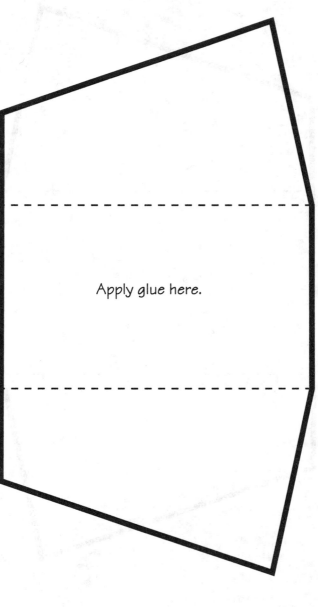

Apply glue here.

Figure and Stand

1. Paste figure and stand onto oaktag.
2. Cut out.
3. Fold stand pattern along dotted lines.
4. Apply glue to stand where indicated.
5. Align stand with bottom of figure and attach.

Apply glue here.

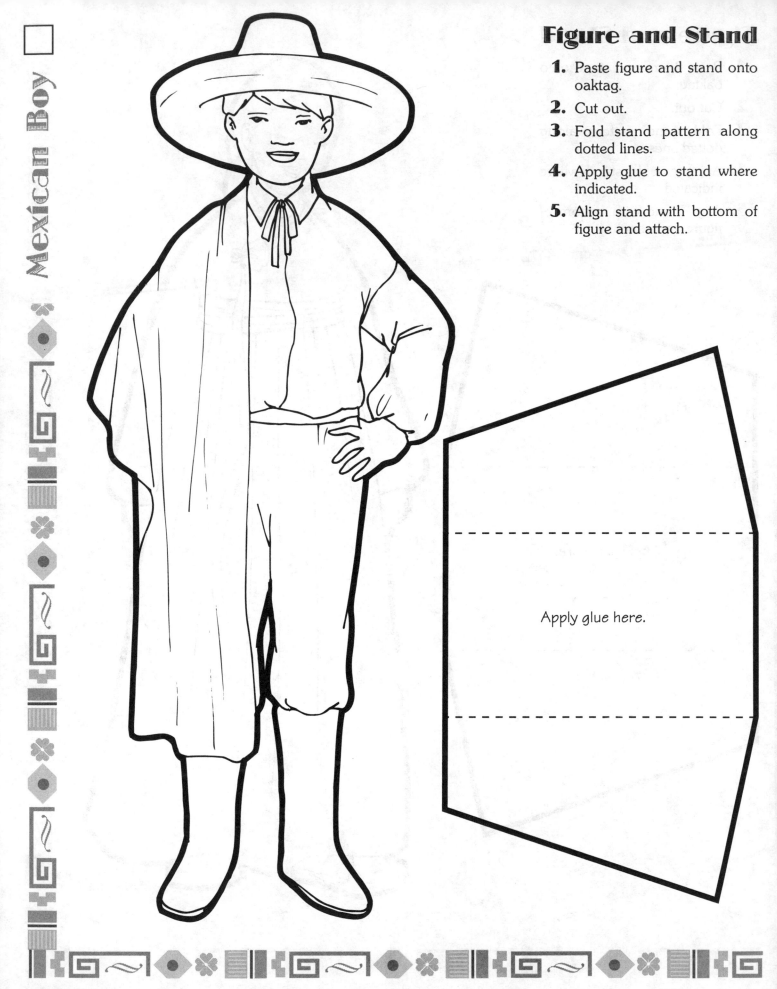

Figure and Stand

1. Paste figure and stand onto oaktag.

2. Cut out.

3. Fold stand pattern along dotted lines.

4. Apply glue to stand where indicated.

5. Align stand with bottom of figure and attach.

Apply glue here.

126

Figure and Stand

1. Paste figure and stand onto oaktag.
2. Cut out.
3. Fold stand pattern along dotted lines.
4. Apply glue to stand where indicated.
5. Align stand with bottom of figure and attach.

Apply glue here.

Mexican Girl

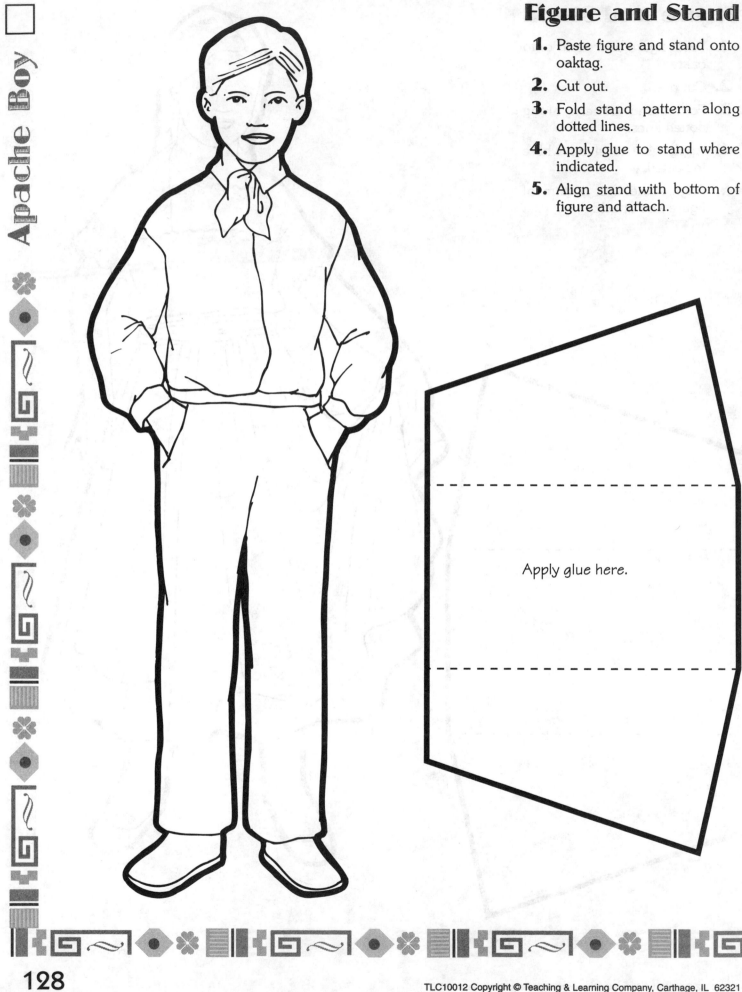

Figure and Stand

1. Paste figure and stand onto oaktag.
2. Cut out.
3. Fold stand pattern along dotted lines.
4. Apply glue to stand where indicated.
5. Align stand with bottom of figure and attach.

Apple glue here.

Apache Boy

Figure and Stand

1. Paste figure and stand onto oaktag.

2. Cut out.

3. Fold stand pattern along dotted lines.

4. Apply glue to stand where indicated.

5. Align stand with bottom of figure and attach.

Apply glue here.

129

Figure and Stand

1. Paste figure and stand onto oaktag.

2. Cut out.

3. Fold stand pattern along dotted lines.

4. Apply glue to stand where indicated.

5. Align stand with bottom of figure and attach.

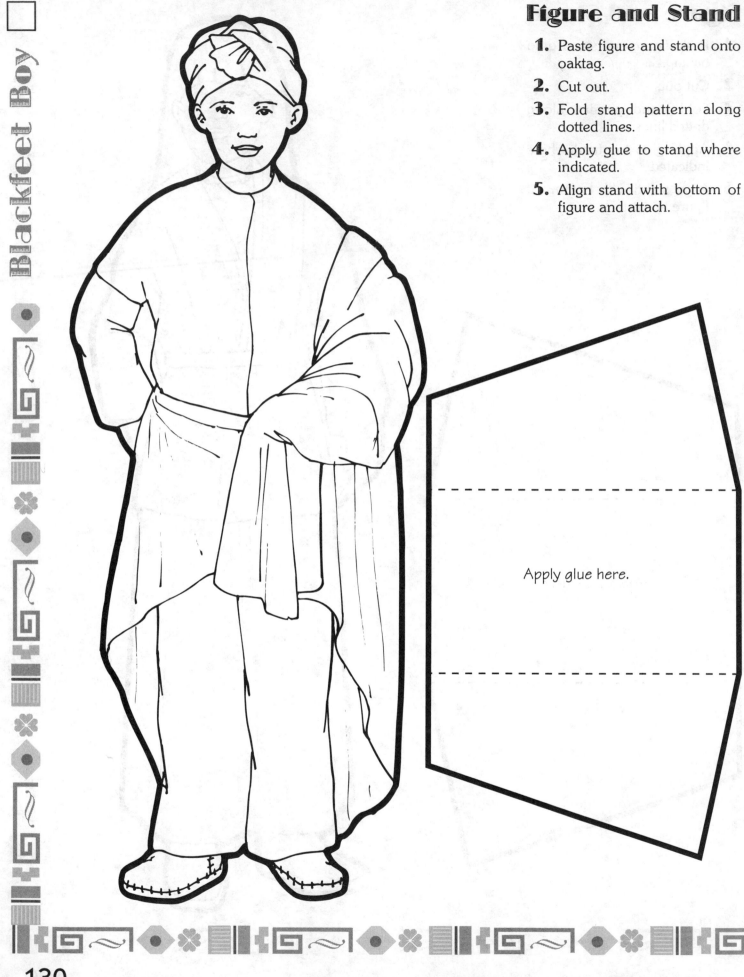

Apply glue here.

Figure and Stand

1. Paste figure and stand onto oaktag.

2. Cut out.

3. Fold stand pattern along dotted lines.

4. Apply glue to stand where indicated.

5. Align stand with bottom of figure and attach.

Apply glue here.

Figure and Stand

1. Paste figure and stand onto oaktag.
2. Cut out.
3. Fold stand pattern along dotted lines.
4. Apply glue to stand where indicated.
5. Align stand with bottom of figure and attach.

Apply glue here.

Figure and Stand

1. Paste figure and stand onto oaktag.

2. Cut out.

3. Fold stand pattern along dotted lines.

4. Apply glue to stand where indicated.

5. Align stand with bottom of figure and attach.

Apply glue here.

Eskimo Girl

Figure and Stand

1. Paste figure and stand onto oaktag.

2. Cut out.

3. Fold stand pattern along dotted lines.

4. Apply glue to stand where indicated.

5. Align stand with bottom of figure and attach.

Apply glue here.

Figure and Stand

1. Paste figure and stand onto oaktag.
2. Cut out.
3. Fold stand pattern along dotted lines.
4. Apply glue to stand where indicated.
5. Align stand with bottom of figure and attach.

Apply glue here.

Multicultural Greeting Cards

Everybody likes to receive greeting cards . . . especially multicultural greeting cards! Invite your students to make and present their own multicultural greeting cards. To get your students started, search local card stores for greeting cards in other languages, or look for cards celebrating the many different cultural holidays. Once you have found the cards you like, ask the students in your class who read or speak foreign languages to translate what's written on the cards. If no one in your class can translate, ask if there is a family member or friend who can help translate the cards for the class. This is a great opportunity to include parents and other adults in your classroom and for children to hear different languages spoken aloud. Now it's time to make your own multicultural greeting cards.

Materials

construction paper   pencils
crayons   markers
greeting cards in many languages

Procedure

1st: Discuss the greeting cards that are in other languages and/or those that commemorate various cultural holidays.

2nd: Ask your students to choose a cultural holiday for their greeting card. They can choose one of the holidays that you have already learned about, or they can choose from those on page 137 or others they have researched or know about.

3rd: Have your students design a card appropriate to the holiday. Hand out construction paper and pencils, crayons or markers. Children in the class or their relatives may be able to translate the messages into the appropriate language. When your students are done, they can exchange or display their cards proudly!

Martin Luther King's Birthday–January 15

Yuan Tan (Chinese New Year)–between January 15 and February 19, the first day of the first moon of the lunar calendar

Maple Festival (an Iroquois celebration with dances and songs)–early spring

International Women's Day (a commeration of women's struggles for justice worldwide)–March 8

Lei Day (a Hawaiian holiday of friendliness and sharing old tales)–May 1

Tet-Trung-Thu (a Vietnamese festival of lanterns to honor the moon)–September or October, the fifth day of the eighth month in the lunar calendar

Bibliography

Albrectsen, L., *Teepee and Moccasin: Indian Crafts for Young People.* New York: Van Nostrand Reinhold, 1972.

Benarde, A., *Games from Many Lands.* New York: The Lion Press, 1970.

Berliner, N.Z., *Chinese Folk Art.* Boston, A New York Graphic Society Book, Little, Brown & Co., 1986.

Grunfeld, F.V., *Games of the World.* Holt, Rinehart and Winston, New York, 1975.

Hamlyn, P., *African Art.* Middlesex, Hamlyn, 1968.

Harvey, M., *Crafts of Mexico.* New York, Macmillan, 1973.

Hunt, S.E., *Games and Sports the World Around.* Third Edition, The Ronald Press Company, New York, 1964.

Joseph, J., *Folk Toys Around the World and How to Make Them.* New York, Parents' Magazine Press, 1972.

Lee, N., and L. Oldham., *Hands-On Heritage.* Hands-On Publications, Long Beach, CA, 1978.

Millen, N., *Children's Festivals from Many Lands.* New York: Friendship Press, 1964.

Purdy, S.G., *Jewish Holidays: Facts, Activities, and Crafts.* New York: J.B. Lippincott Co., 1969.

Saint-Gilles, A., *Mingei: Japan's Enduring Folk Arts.* Heian International, San Francisco, CA, 1983.

Silverthorne, E., *Fiesta! Mexico's Great Celebrations.* The Millbrook Press, Brookfield, CT, 1992.

Supraner, R., *Great Masks to Make.* Troll Asssociates, Mahwah, New Jersey, 1981.